Accessible, engaging, and above
Ken Golden's book is more than
Anyone looking for an introduct
Christian beliefs will find this a

J. Gresham Machen Professor of Theology and Apologetics,
Westminster Seminary California, Escondido, California,
and Founder, White Horse Inn

Thanks to Ken Golden for producing a clear and readable introduction to Reformed theology and Presbyterian polity. This is a resource any pastor should welcome. It will be especially useful for pastors who want to instruct their members, and new members, in the great truths of the gospel, as those truths are expressed in a Presbyterian and Reformed church.

K. Scott Oliphint
Professor of Apologetics and Systematic Theology,
Westminster Theological Seminary,Philadelphia, Pennsylvania

For years our congregation used Calvin Knox Cumming's book *Confessing Christ* for our membership classes. At last a comparable book has been written to replace that now out-of-print classic. Ken Golden's *Presbytopia* takes us through the Christian essentials: from God to man to sin to Christ to the application of redemption (what God has done) to the work of the Spirit (what God is doing). From there we are given a tour of Reformed distinctives: Calvinism, Presbyterian church government, Reformed worship, concluding with the means of grace (preaching, the sacraments, and prayer). Given how rare it is to encounter adequately instructed Christians, never mind Presbyterians, *Presbytopia* is a valuable tool for pastors to use in the new member classes.

Terry L. Johnson
Senior Minister,
Independent Presbyterian Church, Savannah, Georgia

Pastor Ken Golden has provided for all Presbyterians a valuable tool for ministry. As a pastor for 35 years I have written, re-written, edited and amended dozens of Inquirer's Class curriculum. I am a firm believer and am an unashamed advocate of Inquirer's Classes. And not just those that are planned for 4, 5 or 6 weeks, in order to process people into the church quickly with the least amount of information possible. Pastor Golden's material winsomely but thoroughly orients people to the full scope of Presbyterian Faith and Life – its evangelical doctrine and its reformed distinctives. Here is a new member's class unafraid to examine the "fine print" of becoming a Presbyterian. I recommend it to all Presbyterian pastors without their own curriculum, and to all who might ask themselves, "What do those Presbyterians believe anyway?" Read and enjoy the rich content and historically Biblical perspective of this book. Then go find the nearest Presbyterian church and join it!

MIKE ROSS
Senior Pastor, Christ Covenant Church, Matthews, North Carolina

Ken Golden has provided the church with a magnificent resource. Pastor Golden has a sharp theological mind and a love for Christ's church and the ordinary people who inhabit it. This book reflects both of those traits as it takes readers lucidly and winsomely through the basics of Christian faith and practice and introduces them to the life of Reformed churches. I suspect pastors will find it useful not only for acquainting new members with presbyterian ways but also for re-acquainting long-time members with what they've been learning and doing–and helping them to understand why. I heartily recommend this volume for Reformed churches far and wide.

DAVID VANDRUNEN
Robert B. Strimple Professor
of Systematic Theology and Christian Ethics,
Westminster Seminary in California, Escondido, California

PRESBYTOPIA

What it means to be Presbyterian

KEN GOLDEN

Cover Image: The burning bush, a historic symbol of Presbyterian and Reformed churches worldwide.

paperback ISBN 978-1-78191-743-5
epub ISBN 978-1-78191-768-8
mobi ISBN 978-1-78191-769-5

10 9 8 7 6 5 4 3 2 1

Published in 2016
by
Christian Focus Publications Ltd,
Geanies House, Fearn, Ross-shire,
IV20 1TW, Great Britain.

www.christianfocus.com

Cover design by Daniel Van Straaten

Printed and bound
by
Bell & Bain, Glasgow

CONTENTS

PREFACE

I didn't grow up a Presbyterian. My introduction to church membership material came through a class my wife and I attended while I was a student at Westminster Seminary California. The class used Calvin Knox Cummings' helpful book, *Confessing Christ*. After graduating from seminary and teaching membership classes as the pastor of a church, I discovered that there were points I wanted to make that weren't covered in *Confessing Christ*. Consulting additional courses, seminary notes, and other sources, I began to design a class for the church I served. Before long, the class became a labor of love. What you have in your hands is the culmination of far too many hours. It is my hope that this little book will provide some assistance to churches seeking to educate visitors and parishioners alike.

There are many people who deserve some recognition in making this become a reality. As mentioned above, I'm indebted to Rev. Cummings for introducing me to the genre. I'm thankful for my seminary professors who challenged me and deepened my understanding of the Bible. I am grateful for my friends, colleagues, mentors, and parishioners who read versions of this manuscript over the years. In particular, I am much obliged to Michael Matossian and David VanDrunen for their continued support and guidance. I am also appreciative of John van Eyk from Christian Focus for his helpful insights and patient demeanor during the editing process. Finally, I am thankful for my dear wife Cressid and our children, Sam, Joseph, Aaron and Maelah, who have stood by me and exhibited the love of Christ throughout the duration of this project.

BEFORE WE BEGIN

When people visit churches, they come with questions. What do you believe about the Bible? How are you different from the church down the street? Why should I become a member of a Presbyterian Church? These are important questions. And this book is an opportunity to answer such questions. It's an opportunity that may lead to a commitment.

These days church membership has fallen on hard times. Many are content being 'regular attenders' while keeping their options open. While it takes some time finding the right church, the search shouldn't be indefinite. Christianity stresses accountability with a local church and membership is a formal expression of that mutual accountability. It's both a privilege and a responsibility.

In order to become a member of a Presbyterian Church, one must make a credible profession of faith. This means that the interested person must agree with the essential teachings of a Presbyterian church, especially concerning the good news of salvation through faith in Jesus Christ. It also means being committed to the local Presbyterian congregation that embodies these teachings.

The book is titled *Presbytopia*. This brings to mind other 'topias' or places. *Utopia* ('no place') describes an ideal society that's humanly impossible. *Dystopia* ('bad place') suggests a corrupt, even apocalyptic society. Likewise, *Presbytopia*, a made-up word, means 'old place'. This is significant for our generation where old things have fallen on hard times. They're often considered to be outdated and ill-suited for modern life. Even Christians think this way.

But old places have value. Rather than obsolete and out-of-touch, they can be knowledgeable and experienced places, full of old truth that never grows stale. So *Presbytopia* is a place with something to offer. And Presbyterian churches embody such a place.

This book contains what *Presbytopia* has to offer. It's divided into the following three parts:

I. *Christian Essentials*. This is what you must believe in order to make a credible profession of faith.

II. *Reformed Distinctives*. This is also what you will be taught as a member of a Presbyterian church.

III. *Means of Grace*. This is how you will grow as a Christian.

As you read through this book, you will find questions at the end of each chapter for review and discussion. While some chapters translate into sixty to ninety-minute sessions, others require multiple sessions. Welcome to *Presbytopia*!

PART 1
Christian Essentials

INTRODUCTION

The Bible is a big book. It's a book written by different authors living in different times and places. It's full of different literary styles and languages. Clearly, it's a book that requires interpretation. And how we interpret the Bible affects how we teach it. It affects our doctrine.

Not everything in the Bible is easily understood, but there are things that must be understood. These things define what it means to be a Christian. We call these *Christian essentials*. Part 1 presents these essentials under the following categories:

1. Bible – *God's Word to Man*
2. God – *Who He Is*
3. Man – *Who He Was*
4. Sin – *What Man Has Done*
5. Christ – *What God Has Done*
6. Spirit – *Applying What God Has Done*
7. Spirit – *Applying What God Is Doing*

CHAPTER 1

BIBLE
God's Word To Man

The Revelation of God

Before we can talk about the Christian essentials, we need to discuss their source. Where do they come from? The answer is they come from God by means of *revelation*. This describes something that's been disclosed or revealed. Revelation involves communication.

Where does God reveal Himself? He reveals His existence in two places. First He speaks in the natural world. This is called *general revelation*. Think about the vastness of the universe or the complexity of a human body. It's not very likely that such complexity came about by chance; rather it demonstrates a designer. Or think about the universal understanding of a moral code. Most people know the difference between right and wrong. They don't need to be taught that it's wrong to murder and steal. But the question is *why*. Why don't they need to be taught? Why does man act morally while animals act instinctively? Where does this morality come from? It wouldn't be possible if there were no God.

God doesn't only communicate His existence through the natural world. In His perfect wisdom, He has also spoken in the natural world through His supernatural word. This is called *special revelation*. And this form of revelation is found in only one place: the Bible. (Note: Unless otherwise specified, all Biblical references are cited from the English Standard Version.)

Special revelation mentions general revelation. According to Psalm 19:1, 'the heavens declare the glory of God and the sky above proclaims his handiwork'. This explains why the universe itself proclaims a creator. And according to Romans 2:14-15, people are moral creatures because God's law is 'written on their hearts'.

So God reveals Himself clearly in creation, both around and within humanity. He shows Himself so clearly, in fact, that a failure to respond appropriately to this revelation renders man deserving of His judgment. According to the Apostle Paul:

> For the wrath of God is revealed from heaven against all ungodliness and unrighteousness of men, who by their unrighteousness suppress the truth. For what can be known about God is plain to them, because God has shown it to them. For his invisible attributes, namely his eternal power and divine nature, have been clearly perceived, ever since the creation of the world, in the things that have been made. So they are without excuse. (Rom. 1:18-20)

No one can claim innocence. People are inundated with revelation, so they are left without excuse. Choosing to suppress this revelation doesn't remove the guilt. No one is exempt.

But thankfully, special revelation does more than repeat the revelation of God that creation declares. It also reveals God's mercy. The Apostle John explains the reason for his book in these terms: 'But these are written so that you may believe that Jesus is the Christ, the Son of God, and that by believing you may have life in his name' (John 20:31). This is called *the gospel*, the most important thing ever revealed (Rom. 1:16).

The Composition of Scripture

Special Revelation isn't just one book; it's sixty-six books. The Bible is divided into two general parts; the Old and New Testaments. The first part describes 'Christ concealed' (preparation for His arrival), while the second part concerns 'Christ revealed' (His coming and its implications for God's people). Below is a basic division according to content and literary style.

1. Old Testament

a. Pentateuch ('five books'): Genesis, Exodus, Leviticus, Numbers, Deuteronomy. These are a narrative history of God's actions from the beginning to Israel's wilderness wanderings. They include legal and ceremonial writings.

b. Historical Books: Joshua, Judges, Ruth, 1 and 2 Samuel, 1 and 2 Kings, 1 and 2 Chronicles, Ezra, Nehemiah, Esther. These are narrative histories of God's actions from the conquest of Canaan to Israel's exile from the land.

c. Writings: Job, Psalms, Proverbs, Ecclesiastes, Song of Songs. These are a collection of songs and wisdom literature that praise God and describe how to live in relationship with Him.

d. Prophets: Isaiah, Jeremiah, Lamentations, Ezekiel, Daniel, Hosea, Joel, Amos, Obadiah, Jonah, Micah,

Nahum, Habakkuk, Zephaniah, Haggai, Zechariah, Malachi. These are promises, warnings, and predictions for God's people.

2. **New Testament**

   a. *Gospels/Acts*: Matthew, Mark, Luke, John, Acts. These are narrative histories about the life of Jesus Christ and the early church.

   b. *Epistles*: Romans, 1 and 2 Corinthians, Galatians, Ephesians, Philippians, Colossians, 1 and 2 Thessalonians, 1 and 2 Timothy, Titus, Philemon, Hebrews, James, 1 and 2 Peter, 1, 2, 3 John, Jude. These are letters to churches that develop the teaching of Jesus and correct misconceptions.

   c. *Revelation*: This book of image-based prophecy utilizes previous imagery from the Old and New Testaments in order to declare the victory of Christ over His opponents and bring all of Scripture to a close.

The Qualities of Scripture

Knowing what's in the Bible raises other questions. Is the content reliable? Is the information profitable? Here, we seek to answer these questions by discussing how the Bible describes itself.

We begin with *inspiration*. This means that Scripture is *breathed-out* by God (2 Tim. 3:16). While it's true that men wrote the Bible in different times and places, it's also true that God supervised the project. This means that God is the author, even though He used the gifts of many authors. According to the Apostle Peter, 'No prophecy of Scripture comes from someone's own interpretation. For no prophecy was ever produced by the will of man, but men spoke from God as they were carried along by the Holy Spirit' (2 Pet. 1:20-21). This means that God didn't reduce the human writers to mere mechanisms. Instead, He used their unique qualities and historical situations in such a way that their words corresponded to His words.

But this raises another question: Can an inspired book contain errors? The answer, of course, is no. God's inspired word is without error (inerrancy) and cannot be proven wrong (infallibility). Psalm 119:160 says, 'The sum of your word is truth and every one of your righteous rules endures forever'. Here 'truth' equals inerrancy while 'enduring forever' expresses infallibility. This means that the Bible is never wrong and cannot be proven wrong.

That doesn't mean our *interpretations* of the Bible aren't ever wrong. For example, Joshua 10:13 says that the 'sun stood still'. In the past, many read this and believed that the sun rotates around the earth. However, we know from science (general revelation) that the sun doesn't rotate; rather the earth spins and rotates around the sun. So why does Joshua 10:13 say that the sun stood still? The answer is that Joshua 10:13 was written from the standpoint of man's observation. We observe the sun rising and setting, when it's really the earth that's moving. Joshua 10:13 doesn't conflict with Biblical inerrancy. It describes a miracle, but it doesn't explain the miracle with scientific precision.

God's word isn't just true, it's also *powerful*. Genesis 1 shows how God spoke the heavens and the earth into existence. If His word is capable of creating all things from nothing then it's certainly powerful enough to change our lives. 'For the word of God is living and active', says the writer of Hebrews. 'It's sharper than any two-edged sword, piercing to the division of soul and of spirit, of joints and of marrow, and discerning the thoughts and intentions of the heart' (Heb. 4:12). Here, we have a picture of God's word separating what is inseparable. It probes us, exposes us, and changes us. It never returns to God without accomplishing His purpose (Isa. 55:11).

So if Scripture is inspired by God, devoid of error, and powerful enough to change its hearers, then it is a *profitable* word. Paul considers it profitable 'for teaching, for reproof, for correction, and for training in righteousness, so that the man of God may be complete (or mature), equipped for every good work' (2 Tim. 3:16-17). If the Bible is that profitable then we should live our lives according to its teachings.

The Authority of Scripture

Because of these qualities, the Bible is an *authoritative* standard. In fact it's the ultimate standard by which all other standards are measured. What other standards govern our lives? Well, first we are creatures of *reason*. God gave us the ability to think. Besides the ordinary use of the mind, this includes the disciplines of mathematics and philosophy. We are also creatures of *experience*. God gave us senses to test our surroundings. The discipline of science falls into this category. Finally, we are creatures of *tradition*. God gave us common situations and communities that influence our lives. This standard is expressed through cultural institutions, government, and religion. Throughout the book we'll be referring to the Westminster Confession of Faith (WCF), Westminster Larger Catechism (WLC), and Westminster Shorter Catechism (WSC), doctrinal summaries of the Presbyterian tradition.

While these are legitimate standards, they are also fallible standards. Our minds are limited to what we can understand, our senses to what we have discovered, and our traditions to what we have commonly shared. They must be checked against the ultimate standard. The Apostle John expressed this principle in his first epistle: 'Beloved, do not believe every spirit, but test the spirits to see whether they are from God' (1 John 4:1). Whether these 'spirits' are philosophical reflections, scientific theories, or religious doctrines, they need to be judged against the perfect standard of special revelation.

The Completed Standard

For this standard to be perfect, however, it needs to be complete. The Biblical collection (canon) is a closed collection. Neither 'new revelations of the spirit' (e.g., new prophecy) nor 'traditions of men' should be added to it (WCF 1.6).

The Bible alludes to its completion. With the language 'do not add, do not subtract', Deuteronomy 12:32 suggests the closing of the Pentateuch. When Jesus reminded His disciples, 'everything written about me in the Law of Moses and the Prophets and the Psalms must be fulfilled', He was describing the three completed parts of the Old Testament (Luke 24:44-45).

The New Testament also suggests the closing of the canon. Here, it's important to mention the role of the apostles. Jesus gave these 'sent ones' unique authority as His official representatives. 'Whoever receives you receives me, and whoever receives me receives him who sent me' (Matt. 10:40). They in turn commanded future church leaders to guard what was entrusted to them (1 Tim. 6:20) and transmit it to the next generation (2 Tim. 2:2). These apostles and their associates, New Testament prophets, serve as the foundation of the church (Eph. 2:20) because the church is built on the word of Christ (Rom. 10:17). With the passing of these official representatives, the revelation of God is complete.

Testimony also comes from the last book of the Bible. Here, the Apostle John used the language from Deuteronomy 12 to conclude his Revelation:

> I warn everyone who hears the words of the prophecy of this book: if anyone adds to them, God will add to him the plagues described in this book, and if anyone takes away from the words of the book of this prophecy, God will take away his share in the tree of life and in the holy city, which are described in this book (Rev. 22:18-19).

Some may argue that this warning only pertains to the book of Revelation. Nevertheless, 'this book' is the last book in the canon for good reason. It takes previous Biblical images from the Old and New Testaments and brings them to a close. So if we shouldn't add or subtract from this book, then we shouldn't add or subtract from the Bible.

Questions for Review and Discussion

1. What is the difference between general and special revelation?
2. Can general revelation contradict special revelation? What role does interpretation play in understanding how they fit together?
3. What is inspiration?
4. What are inerrancy and infallibility?
5. How is God's word powerful?
6. Why is God's word profitable?
7. What are some standards that govern our lives? Which one judges them all?
8. What is the canon of Scripture and why is it closed? Explain using Biblical texts.

CHAPTER 2

GOD
Who He Is

In our discussion of essential teachings, we begin with God because the Bible begins with God. 'In the beginning, God created the heavens and the earth' (Gen. 1:1). Rather than trying to prove the existence of God, the Bible simply assumes it.

The Attributes of God

Every relationship is built on mutual knowledge. If you want to have a relationship with the God who exists, then you need to know something about Him. The Bible describes God in different ways. It ascribes different qualities or attributes to Him. Since there are so many attributes, we will focus on a few found in WCF Chapter 2.

'Infinite in being and perfection' means having no limits. 'Can you find out the deep things of God? Can you find out the limit of the Almighty?' (Job 11:7). This is a rhetorical question. The answer is 'Of course you can't!' God isn't limited by space (omnipresence). '"Can a man hide himself in secret places so that I cannot see him?" declares the LORD. "Do I not fill heaven and earth?"' (Jer. 23:24). Nor is God limited by time (eternality). Moses mused about this in Psalm 90:1-2: 'Lord, you have been our dwelling place in all generations. Before the mountains were brought forth, or ever you had formed the earth and the world, from everlasting to everlasting you are God.' Infinity, however, goes beyond space and time. God is infinitely knowledgeable, infinitely truthful, and infinitely powerful.

And we shouldn't think that God simply has more knowledge, truthfulness, and power than we have. It's not a matter of quantity, but quality. He is infinitely greater than anything else in the universe. He is the creator and we are mere creatures. And the chasm between the two is wider than we could ever imagine. '"For my thoughts are not your thoughts, neither are your ways my ways," declares the LORD. "For as the heavens are higher than the earth, so are my ways higher than your ways and my thoughts than your thoughts"' (Isa. 55:8-9). The Apostle Paul put it another way:

> Oh, the depth of the riches and wisdom and knowledge of God! How unsearchable are his judgments and how inscrutable his ways! For who has known the mind of the Lord, or who has been his counselor? (Rom. 11:33-34)

The Confession calls this quality *incomprehensible.* It means that God cannot be known exhaustively. And what we can know He makes known through special revelation. Deuteronomy 29:29 explains this important principle: 'The secret things belong to the LORD our God, but the things that are revealed belong to us and to our children forever, that we may do all the words of this law.' As creatures, we cannot know everything about God. Apart from His revelation, we cannot know anything about God. His revelation tells us what we *need* to know.

If God is infinitely powerful, then He has 'sovereign dominion' or full control over all things. As we have seen in Genesis 1:1, God is sovereign in *creation*. He created all things 'out of nothing, by the word of his power, in the space of six days, and all very good' (WSC 9). God is also sovereign in *providence*, 'the preserving and governing of all of his creatures and all of their actions' (WSC 11). He is in such control of nature that not even a sparrow will fall to ground apart from His will (Matt. 10:29). Moreover, He incorporates the actions of men into His sovereign plan. When Joseph revealed his true identity to his brothers who had sold him into slavery, they were expecting the worst. Instead, he taught them something about God's providence:

> And God sent me before you to preserve for you a remnant on earth, and to keep alive for you many survivors. So it was not you who sent me here, but God. ... You meant evil against me, but God meant it for good. (Gen. 45:7-8; 50:20)

Here, the providence of God extends to wicked men without participating in their wicked actions. If this were the case, it would violate another one of His attributes. He is 'most holy' which means perfect and pure, set apart from all creation.

The prophet Isaiah was an eyewitness to the holiness of God. He saw the Lord sitting on a throne, with heavenly attendants crying out, 'Holy, holy, holy is the LORD of hosts; the whole earth is full of his glory!' How did this prophet respond to such glory? 'Woe is me! For I am lost; for I am a man of unclean lips and I dwell in the midst of a people of unclean lips; for my eyes have seen the King, the LORD of hosts!' (Isa. 6:3-5). Isaiah recognized his lack of holiness when confronted by a God of infinite holiness. Such an encounter spells doom for the lesser party!

God's holiness is inseparable from His righteousness. The confession declares Him to be 'most just, and terrible in his judgments hating all sin, and who will by no means clear the guilty' (WCF 2.1). Since God is infinitely righteous, He demands perfect obedience to His Law. Here the scene shifts from temple to courtroom. 'The heavens declare his righteousness,' writes Asaph, 'for God himself is judge' (Ps. 50:6). 'Clouds and thick darkness are all around him; righteousness and justice are the foundation of his throne,' warns another writer (Ps. 97:2). Such a God shouldn't be taken lightly. There is no room for disobedience to His commands. He must punish the guilty.

A most holy and righteous God is hardly approachable. Isaiah found that out the hard way. These moral qualities, however, do not exhaust His attributes. God is also 'most loving' – the greatest attribute communicated to man (see 1 Cor. 13). Indeed, God not only loves, but God is the very principle of love (1 John 4:8).

The Trinity

This last attribute raises a few questions. How can God embody love when love is relational? How could He love before He created objects of love? Well, there's another attribute that shows God's love from all eternity. We call it the mystery of the *Trinity* – one God in three persons.

The Bible speaks of one God. Moses said, 'Hear, O Israel: The LORD our God, the LORD is one' (Deut. 6:4) while Jesus said, 'I and the Father are one' (John 10:30). And this one God also reveals Himself in three persons. After Jesus was baptized in the Jordan River, the gospel writer Mark describes the interaction between the three persons of the Trinity in these words:

> When he came up out of the water, immediately he saw the heavens being torn open and the Spirit descending on him like a dove. And a voice came from heaven, 'You are my beloved Son; with you I am well pleased' (Mark 1:10-11).

Here, the participants aren't three separate gods (tri-theism), for that would destroy their 'oneness'. Nor are they three appearances of the same God (modalism), for that would destroy their unique personalities and make the story nonsensical. Instead, we see three *persons* – who are all one God – interacting with each other. Just because we can't fully wrap our minds around it doesn't make it any less true.

We have already seen how the Father spoke to Jesus at His baptism. Throughout the gospels, Jesus conversed with Him and told others about their relationship. While the divinity of Father has always been accepted, the divinity of the Son is another matter. There are groups today who deny the deity of Christ, but the Bible is not on their side. The following statements about Jesus provide sufficient testimony to this truth. 'In the beginning was the Word and the Word was with God and the Word was God' (John 1:1). 'For in him the whole fullness of the deity dwells bodily' (Col. 2:9). 'He is the radiance of the glory of God and the exact imprint of his nature' (Heb. 1:3). Identifying Himself with God's self-disclosure, 'I am who I am' (Exod. 3:14), Jesus made the following claims about Himself: 'I am the bread of life' (John 6:48), 'I am the light of the world' (John 8:12), 'I am the resurrection and the life' (John 11:25), 'Before Abraham was, I am' (John 8:58).

The Apostle John, in particular, leaves us without any doubt about the divinity of Jesus in the Book of Revelation. First he recorded, '"I am the Alpha and the Omega," says the Lord God, "who is and who was and who is to come, the Almighty"' (Rev. 1:8). Then upon seeing 'one like a son of man' in a vision, he 'fell at his feet as though dead' (Rev. 1:13, 17a). This reminds us of Isaiah's experience, the typical reaction to seeing God through impure eyes. John's vision, however, wasn't finished: 'But he laid his right hand on me, saying, "Fear not, I am the first and the last, and the living one. I died, and behold I am alive forevermore, and I have the keys of Death and Hades"' (Rev. 1:17b-18). Notice how the 'son of man' used the same language as the Lord God to describe Himself (e.g., 'I am the Alpha and the Omega') with one exception: He also mentioned that He *died.* God the Father never died, but His Son Jesus Christ died on the Cross and was raised from the dead. What does this mean? It means that John encountered Jesus in his vision. It means that Jesus is the Eternal One, even the Infinite One. He is God.

Why is this important? It matters a great deal in the plan of salvation, but for now it serves a specific purpose: the Son reveals the Father to His people. We wouldn't know God and His salvation if Jesus hadn't come. He said as much in John 14:6-7:

> I am the way, and the truth, and the life. No one comes to the Father except through me. If you had known me, you would have known my Father also. From now on you do know him and have seen him.

For centuries, people have desired to see God. The countless statues and images that fill our museums testify to this truth. Jesus, however, had a different answer for His disciples: 'If you want to see God, you're looking right at him!'

So the Father is God and the Son is God. Yet there is still one more person in the Trinity. He is called the Holy Spirit. Some groups consider Him nothing more than a force, but the Bible doesn't support such an idea. When the Apostle Peter confronted Ananias about his deception, he mentioned this specific person of the Trinity. He said, 'Ananias, why has Satan filled your heart to lie to the Holy Spirit and to keep back for yourself part of the proceeds of the land? ... You have not lied to men but to God' (Acts 5:3-4). Notice that Peter specifically referred to the Spirit as God. Also notice that he considered the Spirit a *person*. Only a person can be lied to and only a person can be grieved (Eph. 4:30). The Spirit is just as personal as the Father and the Son.

But isn't it enough to have the Father and the Son? Why do we need the Spirit? Again, this will be discussed in more detail, but for now He serves a specific purpose: the Spirit reveals the Son to His people. Jesus said, 'But when the Helper comes, whom I will send to you from the Father, the Spirit of Truth, who proceeds from the Father, he will bear witness about me' (John 15:26). Paul reminded his readers that 'no one can say "Jesus is Lord" except in the Holy Spirit' (1 Cor. 12:3).

The Trinity is essential in understanding who God is. The problem is that many Christians don't know what to do with it. Many regard it as intellectual dogma with few practical benefits. As we will see, the Trinity isn't some irrelevant doctrine to be acknowledged and then ignored. Rather, it describes God's love from all eternity, three persons working together for the good of God's people, demonstrated in the gospel.

Questions for Review and Discussion

1. What are the attributes of God?
2. What does it mean for God to be infinite? Describe different aspects of this attribute.
3. What does it mean for God to be incomprehensible?

4. What does God's sovereign dominion describe? Provide examples from nature and history.
5. What does it mean for God to be most holy? How does this attribute affect those who are not most holy?
6. What does it mean for God to be most righteous? What are His expectations for law-keeping?
7. What does it mean for God to be most loving? What is the eternal expression of this attribute?
8. What is the Trinity?
9. How is the Son divine? What purpose does He serve?
10. How is the Spirit divine and a person? What purpose does He serve?

Chapter **3**

MAN
Who He Was

In the last chapter, we learned that God has sovereign dominion in creation. Genesis 1 offers a profound look at the days of creation. It chronicles how God separated the light from the darkness, the waters above and below the expanse, and dry land from the sea. It describes God populating the sky with flying creatures, the sea with swimming creatures, and the land with creeping things, domesticated animals, and wild beasts. But the highlight of the week would come on day six with the creation of a most unusual creature.

The Image of God

What does it mean to be human? At the most basic level, man is a creature; humans were created by God. But man is more than a mere creature. Humanity is not a species. Man is the *climax* of God's creation. Animals were brought forth by the earth (Gen. 1:24; 2:19), but God formed man from the dust of the ground and breathed into his nostrils the breath of life (Gen. 2:7). This is different, even intimate. Animals were made 'according to their kind' (Gen. 1:11-12, 21, 24-25), but man was made in the *image of God* (Gen. 1:26).

Does this mean that we look like God? The answer is no. Jesus Christ is called the image of the *invisible* God (Col. 1:15). Paul described the Lord as one 'who dwells in unapproachable light, whom no one has ever seen or can see' (1 Tim. 6:16).

Then how can man be called His image? The simple answer is that mankind reflects aspects of God's attributes to the lesser creation. But the image shouldn't be reduced to a collection of intellectual and moral qualities. In Genesis 5:1-3, the language of 1:26-27 is repeated, with one surprising addition: the first man fathered a son in his own likeness after his image. Since his image is God's image, this makes him God's child (cf. Luke 3:38). This offers a profound insight into the nature of man. Rather than creating us as a higher species than the animals, God makes us His children. We're created according to *His* kind.

With privileges come responsibilities. As a son of God, man was created to *know* his heavenly father. In Genesis 2:16-17, we are told that the Lord God commanded the man. This implies that a conversation was taking place. God was the subject and man was the object. Man received the word of God directly from the mouth of God.

But that's not all. Man was also created to *rule* the lesser creation. Psalm 47:2 calls the Lord 'a great king over the earth', and yet He appointed man to 'have dominion' over the lesser creatures (Gen. 1:26). Man was designated as a lesser king who would rule on God's behalf on earth. Just as God named the light 'day,' the darkness 'night,' the dry land 'earth,' and the waters 'seas' (Gen. 1:5, 9, 10), man named the animals (and even the woman) as an act of dominion (Gen. 2:19, 23). Just as the Lord multiplied the lesser creatures (Gen. 1:22), so man was commissioned to 'be fruitful and multiply, fill the earth and subdue it' (Gen. 1:28).

Man, however, had one more task. He was created to work and guard the holy place of God. Now most of our translations say that 'the LORD God took the man and put him in the Garden of Eden to work it and keep it' (Gen. 2:15). The Hebrew word for 'keep' can also mean 'guard'. This is exactly what it means in Genesis 3:24, where the Lord drove out the man and replaced him with cherubim and a flaming sword 'that turned every way to guard the way to the tree of life' (Gen. 3:24). Later temples in the Old Testament also contained images of cherubim and trees (Exod. 25:18-20; 1 Kings 6:28, 29, 32, 35), reflecting back on the original temple of God. This implies that man had *something* to guard and conversely, something to ward off.

The Covenant of Works

Besides these responsibilities, God also gave His image-bearer a goal. Man was created to enter into God's eternal rest symbolized by the Sabbath (Gen. 2:1-3; Heb. 4:4-11). And this goal would be achieved by means of *covenant*. What is a covenant? Simply put, it's a legal relationship. Marriage is an example of a covenant between two people (Mal. 2:14). Ancient Near Eastern covenant treaties involved blessings for obedience and curses for disobedience (Deut. 28). While the *concept* of covenants might be unfamiliar to many Christians, the *content* of covenants – two in particular – is essential to Christianity. This chapter introduces the first of these two covenants between God and man.

God made His first covenant with Adam, the first man (Hosea 6:7). This was called the *covenant of works*. By keeping this covenant, Adam had the potential to earn eternal life for himself and his descendants. Besides the responsibilities that God gave him as image-bearer, Adam was given a test. It involved two trees: the tree of life and the tree of the knowledge of good and evil. God forbade Adam to eat of the second tree and punctuated His command with an ominous curse: 'for in the day that you eat of it you shall surely die' (Gen. 2:17). This curse, however, suggests that the opposite would also be true. If Adam does not eat of the tree of the knowledge of good and evil then he would earn the right to eat of the tree of life, a sign and seal of eternal life (Gen. 3:22; Rev. 2:7). This would involve more than a continuation of his present state in the garden. It would cause a transition from innocence to glory. Mankind would enter into its ultimate state where all thoughts and actions would be informed by a perfect love for God.

The test, however, was not so easy; it also involved a catalyst. 'Now the serpent was more crafty than any other beast of the field that the LORD God had made' (Gen. 3:1). How was it more crafty? Well for one thing it could talk! But even more important is the force behind the serpent. Revelation 12:9 identifies this 'ancient serpent' with the names Devil (slanderer) and Satan (enemy). Jesus called him 'a murderer from the beginning' and 'the father of all lies' (John 8:44). This is the agent of temptation who would challenge Adam's loyalty to the covenant. Ultimately it would challenge man to decide between two sources of revelation: the word of the Lord and the word of the serpent.

This challenge centered on the second tree, where knowledge of good and evil involved the right of obtaining such knowledge. At stake was nothing less than the relationship between God as creator and man as His creature. Man was already God's image-bearer. Adam was already receiving special revelation from the Lord. Therefore, eating of this tree would involve a desire to gain knowledge beyond the revelation of God – secret knowledge secured through human autonomy. Ultimately, man would no longer be content as a creature. He would strive to be like God in an inappropriate way.

So what happened in the covenant of works? How did Adam fare in his probation? Genesis 3 picks up the story:

> [The serpent] said to the woman, 'Did God actually say, "You shall not eat of any tree in the garden?"' And the woman said to the serpent, 'We may eat of the fruit of the trees in the garden, but God said, "You shall not eat of the fruit of the tree that is in the midst of the garden, neither shall you touch it, lest you die".' But the serpent said to the woman, 'You will not surely die. For God knows that when you eat of it your eyes will be opened, and you will be like God, knowing good and evil' (Gen. 3:1-5).

Notice how the serpent went around God's authority structure to tempt the woman. She was created to complement man and be his helpmate (Gen. 2:20-25), not to represent the covenant family in dealings with talking serpents! Notice how the serpent created doubt ('Did God actually say?') and outright lied ('You will not surely die').

Of course, this raises the question: Where was Adam? As it turns out, he's been there the whole time! 'So when the woman saw that the tree was good for food, and that it was a delight to the eyes, and that the tree was to be desired to make one wise, she took of its fruit and ate, and *she also gave some to her husband who was with her, and he ate*' (Gen. 3:6). Notice how Adam failed on all accounts. He didn't guard the sanctuary from the intruder. He didn't guard his wife from the intruder. And worst of all, he listened to the word of the serpent instead of the word of God. He failed the test and broke the covenant of works. Something was about to change between God and His image-bearers and that something was sin.

Questions for Review and Discussion

1. What is the image of God? What are some characteristics of being an image-bearer?
2. What was the goal of mankind? By what means would man achieve this goal?
3. What is a covenant?
4. Describe the covenant of works. What did it involve? Who were the parties? Who was the catalyst? What were the blessings and curses?
5. Why did the serpent approach the woman?
6. Did Adam succeed in meeting the requirements of the covenant of works? Why or why not?

CHAPTER 4

SIN
What Man Has Done

Adam was in big trouble. He was given the task of guarding the garden from the likes of the serpent. He was given the responsibility of shepherding his wife. What's more, he was given the capacity to keep the covenant of works. Sadly, he failed on all accounts and was expelled from Eden. And worst of all, his failure meant consequences for us all. Sin, you see, entered the world through Adam.

What is sin? In a nutshell, sin is a violation of God's law. It's not doing what you should do or doing what you shouldn't do (WSC 14). And it's not just some minor infraction. First John 3:4 considers it the essence of lawlessness. It's an assault on the righteousness of God. We were created to obey His law, and as James reminds us, 'Whoever keeps the whole law but fails in one point has become accountable for all of it' (James 2:10). God doesn't grade on a curve; it's all or nothing. The bad news is that imperfect law-keeping equals sin.

And for those who think they can achieve perfect law-keeping, sin involves more than what we do. It's what we think and how we speak. Jesus expands our thinking by considering bitterness a form of murder (Matt. 5:21-22) and lust a form of adultery (Matt. 5:27-28).

The consequences of sin are serious. For Adam and Eve, it immediately led to *guilt*. After eating the forbidden fruit, their eyes were opened, but what did they see? Did they experience deep and mysterious truths? No, they discovered something about themselves, something they hadn't noticed before – their nakedness. The point is not that they were nude, but *uncovered*. They realized that they were naked before a holy and righteous God.

So what did they do to fix the problem? They made a covering. They sewed fig leaves together and made themselves loincloths (Gen. 3:7). They tried to cover up their guilt.

They didn't succeed. The Lord found them hiding in fear. He asked the man, 'Where are you?' What was Adam's answer? 'I heard the sound of you in the garden, and I was afraid, because I was naked, and I hid myself.' God responded, 'Who *told* you that you were naked? Have you eaten of the tree of which I commanded you not to eat?' Now listen to Adam's answer: 'The woman whom *you* gave to be with me, *she* gave me fruit of the tree, and I ate.' And when God asked the woman about her actions, she minimized, 'The serpent deceived me, and I ate.' Did you notice the blame-shifting? The man blamed the woman and the woman blamed the serpent. But it's worse than that. The man indirectly blamed God for giving him the woman! Here, guilt led to a refusal to take responsibility. And the fruit of this failure was *alienation,* hiding from God and blaming each other.

There were more consequences for Adam and his wife. Sin would also lead to *suffering*. Now women would experience the pains of childbearing (Gen. 3:16). Even their greatest joy would involve great pain. Man, on the other hand, would experience the common curse. The Lord's creation that was declared 'very good' (Gen. 1:31) would now yield crops only through hard labor (Gen. 3:17-19). By the sweat of his face, man would battle through the thorns and thistles to provide for his family. Man was created to have dominion over the earth, but now the earth would not submit to his rule.

What could be worse? How about death? By breaking the covenant, Adam earned the curse of the covenant. Made from the dust, he would return to the dust (Gen. 3:19). While God created His image-bearer to earn eternal life, by sin he earned the wages of death (Rom. 6:23).

Adam and his wife faced steep consequences for their actions, but the consequences extend to their descendants as well. Adam's sin impacts all of mankind. It affects us because Adam was the federal representative of the human race. A modern example is a president's connection to his nation. If the president declares war on a foreign nation, then all of his citizens are at war with that foreign nation because he represents them in this matter. On the field of battle, the foreign soldiers wouldn't make distinctions between the president's supporters and critics; all would be regarded as the enemy. In a similar way, the human race is connected to Adam. Acting on our behalf, he declared war against God by siding with the serpent. His failure to keep the covenant is deemed to be our failure. This is so important that Paul repeatedly made this point in Romans chapter 5:

- 'Therefore, just as sin came into the world through one man, and death through sin, and so death spread to all men because all sinned.' (v. 12)
- 'For if many died through one man's trespass ...' (v. 15)

- 'For the judgment following one trespass brought condemnation ...' (v. 16)
- 'Therefore as the one trespass led to condemnation for all men ...' (v. 18)
- 'For as by the one man's disobedience the many were made sinners ...' (v. 19)

We're not responsible for all of Adam's sins, just the first one. That one was *imputed* to us, credited to our account. It's just as if we sinned along with him. That's why we call it 'original sin'.

Adam's sin also makes us *polluted*. It corrupted our nature so that we are now disposed towards sin. Job put it this way: 'Man who is born of a woman is few of days and full of trouble. ... Who can bring a clean thing out of an unclean? There is not one' (Job 14:1, 4). After Adam, there is no one who does not sin. 'For all have sinned and fall short of the glory of God' (Rom. 3:23).

Guilty and polluted by sin, the legacy of mankind is death. Death, however, is not only physical. It's more than a separation of the soul from the body. It must also be understood as spiritual. This form of death is the common affliction of mankind. There are many people walking the earth today who are dead in their trespasses and sins (Eph. 2:1). Despite their ability to think and act, they have no interest in or inclination towards God.

This is bad news, but it gets even worse. Death, you see, isn't the ultimate destination. Contrasting the fear of physical death with an even graver consequence, Jesus said to His disciples:

> I tell you, my friends, do not fear those who kill the body, and after that have nothing more that they can do. But I

> will warn you whom to fear: fear him who, after he has killed, has authority to cast into hell. Yes, I tell you, fear him! (Luke 12:4-5).

Hell is a place where sinners will experience the wrath of God, not for a time, but for eternity (Matt. 25:46). It's depicted as a fiery furnace or an outer darkness characterized by 'weeping and gnashing of teeth' (Matt. 13:50; 22:13). The Book of Revelation pictures the serpent, his minions, and 'everyone whose name is not written in the book of life' in a lake of fire 'where they will be tormented day and night forever and ever' (Rev. 19:20; 20:10, 15).

All sin deserves this punishment. It's what we've earned through our thoughts, attitudes, and actions. This is really bad news.

Questions for Review and Discussion

1. What is sin? What does it involve?
2. What is the implication of Adam and his wife's nakedness? What did they do about it?
3. How did sin affect the relationships in the Garden of Eden?
4. In what ways does Adam's sin affect us? Discuss original sin.
5. Discuss other consequences of sin. Explain what is worse than death.

CHAPTER 5

CHRIST
What God Has Done

Sin has left mankind in a terrible state. Under such circumstances, how can we be saved from certain judgment? The answer is that only God can save us. He does so through the making of another covenant.

The Covenant of Grace

The covenant of grace differs from the covenant of works. It's God's promise of salvation for those who place their faith in the *covenant mediator*. Jesus Christ is called 'the mediator between God and man' (1 Tim. 2:5) and 'the guarantor of a better covenant' (Heb. 7:22). This is not simply an arbitrator between two hostile parties, but a reconciler who takes responsibility for the covenant, even at the cost of His own life.

In order to accomplish this, the covenant mediator needed to accomplish three things. First, He who already existed as God needed to take on human nature, becoming the God-man. This is called the *incarnation*. Second, He needed to keep the Law perfectly for the sake of His people. In this capacity He is deemed the *second Adam*. Finally, He needed to offer His own life for the sins of His people. In doing this, He served as the *substitutionary sacrifice*.

We get the first glimpse of this covenant in Genesis 3:15. After exposing the sins of our first parents, the Lord pronounced a curse on the serpent: 'I will put enmity between you and the woman, and between your offspring and her offspring; he shall bruise your head, and you shall bruise his heel'. This text has been called the *proto-evangel* because it's the first (proto) time the gospel (evangel) was pronounced before the coming of Christ. Here, we have a preview of the historical struggle between the forces of the Lord and the forces of the serpent that culminate in the struggle between Jesus and Satan. The prophecy finds its ultimate fulfillment on the cross. There, the serpent's 'head' would be bruised in complete defeat. There, the savior's 'heel' would be bruised through suffering and death.

How did Adam respond to the proto-evangel? He responded in faith. He renamed his wife 'Eve' which means 'mother of all living'. (Gen. 3:20). Just as death has a physical and spiritual meaning, so also does life. Adam and Eve were already alive in a physical sense; but by believing in the proto-evangel, they show themselves to be spiritually alive and inheritors of the promise.

God also responded to Adam's faith with a gracious gesture of His own. In verse 21 we are told that He made 'garments of skins and clothed them'. This is important for three reasons. First, it reveals that sin must be covered for man to have a relationship with God. Second, it shows that by grace, God replaces man's inadequate covering (the fig leaves) with a covering of His choosing. Finally, it demonstrates that God's superior covering is costly. Animal skins imply the death of a creature. Something had to die for man to be reconciled with God. This involved a sacrifice – payment for sin.

The God-Man

The covenant of grace required the mediator to take on human nature. In the incarnation, the second person of the Trinity added to Himself a human nature which resulted in God and man becoming one person. 'In the beginning was the Word, and the Word was with God, and the Word was God' (John 1:1), but at a certain point in history, 'the Word became flesh and dwelt among us' (John 1:14). This 'God-man' was conceived by the power of the Holy Spirit (Luke 1:35) and born of the Virgin Mary (Luke 2:7). He grew; increasing in wisdom and stature (Luke 2:52). He endured, experiencing hunger and thirst (Matt. 4:2; John 19:28), sadness and exhaustion (John 11:35; 4:6). He experienced the human condition with one notable exception: though tempted in every way that we are tempted, He was without sin (Heb. 4:15).

The divine and human natures of the person of Jesus are necessary for salvation because they overcome two challenges. The first challenge concerns God's infinite nature. If man sins against an infinite God then he cannot make payment due to his limitations. The Psalmist recognized this fact. He conceded that 'no man can ransom another, or give to God the price of his life, for the ransom of their life is costly and can never suffice, that he should live on forever and never see the pit' (Ps. 49:7-9). No man can do this, but the God-man can. As God, Jesus can achieve what is impossible for man. He can offer a sacrifice of infinite value for the sins of His people.

Yet being God wasn't enough. Man sinned against God, so it would take another man to make things right. Jesus had to be fully human so that He could represent His people before the Father. According to Hebrews 2:17, 'he had to be made like his brothers in every respect, so that he might become a merciful and faithful high priest in the service of God, to make propitiation for the sins of the people'. For Jesus to represent His people and turn away the wrath of His Father, He needed to be human. His sacrifice needed to be both infinite and representative.

The Second Adam

Before He could make propitiation, however, Jesus needed to accomplish what His people were incapable of accomplishing. He needed to keep the law in their place. He needed to come as a *second Adam*, the federal or representative head of a new human race.

Both Adams were born with a mission: perfect obedience to the Law. The first Adam needed to keep the covenant of works to earn eternal life for himself and his descendants, but he failed. The second Adam, however, kept the covenant of works so that His people would inherit eternal life. For Jesus, the covenant of grace was essentially a covenant of works.

Both Adams experienced a test. For the first Adam, it involved the serpent in the garden. He failed the test by choosing the word of the serpent over the word of God. The second Adam, however, encountered the serpent in the wilderness (Luke 4:1-13). There, in a physically weaker state than the first Adam, He countered the words of the serpent with the word of God.

But the temptations didn't end in the wilderness. They continued throughout His ministry. On the eve of His death, in another garden, with the Cross drawing near and His Father's wrath looming large, the second Adam cried out these words to His Father: 'If you are willing, remove this [wrathful] cup from me'. But this Adam didn't succumb to the temptation of disobedience; rather, He submitted to the plan of His Father: 'nevertheless, not my will, but yours, be done' (Luke 22:42).

Why was it necessary for Jesus to be the second Adam? The first Adam represented all of his people, so when he sinned, *we all* sinned. Likewise, the second Adam represented all of His people, so when He obeyed God's Law perfectly, His people receive the credit. Paul wrote, 'For as by the one man's disobedience the many were made sinners, so by the one man's obedience the many will be made righteous' (Rom. 5:19). Only through Christ's work, can we be considered righteous before God who is 'most just, and terrible in his judgments' (WCF 2.1).

The Substitutionary Sacrifice

Even though Christ kept the Law on behalf of His people, there's still one problem: His people are *sinners*. Something still has to be done about their sin. In the Old Testament, sin was covered through sacrifice. We already saw how God provided animal skins to cover the sins of Adam and Eve. In Exodus 12, the Lord instructed the Israelites to slaughter unblemished lambs and wipe their blood on the door-posts of their homes. He would kill the firstborn Egyptians, but spare the firstborn Israelites whose homes were covered by the blood. Here we have an example of a sacrificial covering that turned away (propitiated) the wrath of God. The sacrifice provided a substitute for the sins of Israel. After the Exodus, sacrificial substitution was institutionalized in the Book of Leviticus.

This system, however, was not an end in itself. The writer of Hebrews explains this as follows:

> For since the law has but a shadow of the good things to come instead of the true form of these realities, it can never, by the same sacrifices that are continually offered every year, make perfect those who draw near. Otherwise, would they not have ceased to be offered, since the worshipers, having once been cleansed, would no longer have any consciousness of sins? But in these sacrifices there is a reminder of sins every year. For it is impossible for the blood of bulls and goats to take away sins. (Heb. 10:1-4)

This shows us that the animal sacrifices were not the final solution. How could they be? They lacked infinite value and true representational character. Instead, they pointed to something greater than themselves, something that could deal with sin once for all. In the New Testament, the ultimate sacrifice comes in the person and work of Jesus Christ. Again, Hebrews says:

> Consequently when Christ came into the world, he said 'Sacrifices and offerings you have not desired, but a body have you prepared for me; in burnt offerings and sin offerings you have taken no pleasure. Then I said, "Behold, I have come to do your will, O God, as it is written of me in the scroll of the book"' (Heb. 10:5-7).

Why didn't God desire these sacrifices? Didn't He command Israel to offer them? While these sacrifices reminded Israel of the need for covering, they were not offered of their own volition. The animals didn't choose to be sacrificed! Jesus offered Himself *voluntarily*. His will was in harmony with His Father's will, so His sacrifice was a desirable sacrifice. Moreover, the very nature of those sacrifices was insufficient since they were finite and animal. On the other hand, Jesus does away with all the previous sacrifices of the Old Covenant once and for all (Heb. 10:8-10).

Some may wonder if this is too complicated. Why all this need for sacrifice? It's necessary because divine justice requires perfect obedience to the law. To show this, we need to ask ourselves a question: Is there anything that God can't do? At first blush, we might say 'no' until we think about His attributes. For example, it is impossible for God to lie (Heb. 6:18). The same holds true for His righteousness. Just as it's impossible for a God of truth to lie, so it's impossible for a God of righteousness to overlook sin (Exod. 34:7).

But lest we forget, the Lord is more than a God of righteousness; He is also God of mercy. How can He show mercy without denying His righteousness? By providing a substitute! His justice demands the shedding of blood (Heb. 9:22), while His mercy offers the sacrifice of His Son (Heb. 2:17).

The Resurrection

The cross wasn't good news for the disciples of Jesus. For them it symbolized defeat. Their dreams of a resurgent Israel under the banner of the Christ were shattered by His death. On the road to Emmaus, a couple of them admitted, 'we had hoped that he was the one to redeem Israel' (Luke 24:21). What changed their perspective? What caused them to come out of hiding and boldly proclaim the gospel of the cross? The answer is the resurrection.

The disciples were wrong. The cross was good news for sinners, but it required another event to make it effective. God validated this once-for-all sacrifice by raising His Son from the dead. The Apostle Paul wrote that Jesus 'was delivered up for our trespasses and raised for our justification.' (Rom. 4:25) Here we see how the crucifixion and resurrection are inseparable. He was raised from the dead so we could be right with God.

Being raised from the dead also means that Christ has *conquered* death; it has lost its grip on His people (1 Cor. 15:55). Mankind wasn't created to die, but to live forever. By being raised from the dead, Jesus shows us that the curse of death has been defeated. Therefore, His people have no reason to fear.

Moreover, Paul connects Christ's resurrection with our future resurrections. In 1 Corinthians 15:20-23, he began by comparing the two Adams: death came through the first, but resurrection resulted from the second. Then, he showed that Christ's resurrection was the *first fruits* (first yield) of a harvest of resurrections. Since He was resurrected from the dead, His disciples will also be resurrected from the dead. Christians can know for certain that they will receive bodies that will never perish as they glorify God for the rest of eternity.

Since Paul's day, there have been people who question the importance of the resurrection. To such people, Paul didn't sugar-coat his answer:

> If Christ has not been raised, your faith is futile and you are still in your sins. Then those also who have fallen asleep in Christ have perished. If in Christ we have hope in this life only, we are of all people most to be pitied (1 Cor. 15:17-19).

These are harsh words for skeptical ears. So-called 'spiritual resurrections' and other solutions that deny this physical component of salvation are rejected. The resurrection of Christ stands at the core of the Christian faith, a doctrine joyfully confessed by those who share in His victory.

Questions for Review and Discussion

1. What is the Covenant of Grace? What was required of its guarantor? Where did it originate?
2. What is the Incarnation? Why is it necessary for salvation?
3. How did Christ fill the role of being the second Adam? Why is this necessary for salvation?
4. Explain the role of sacrifices in the Old Testament. How was Christ the ultimate substitutionary sacrifice? Why is His sacrifice necessary for salvation?
5. What did the resurrection accomplish?

CHAPTER **6**

SPIRIT
Applying What God Has Done

In the last chapter we learned what Jesus has done for us. How then do we receive the benefits of His work? After all, we are separated from His work by *space*. He's in heaven, while we're still on earth. We are also separated from His work by *time*. He lived in the first century, but we live in the twenty-first century. The answer is that God isn't limited by space and time. He sends the Holy Spirit to apply the work of salvation to us.

Despite the primary emphasis on Christ, the Spirit isn't a bit player in Christianity. He was involved in the work of creation, hovering over the face of the primeval deep (Gen. 1:2). He was involved in the accomplishment of redemption, overshadowing the womb of the virgin, conceiving the human nature of Christ (Luke 1:35), empowering Jesus throughout His ministry (Mark 1:10, 12) and effecting His resurrection (Rom. 1:4; 1 Pet. 3:18). He also applies the benefits of redemption to God's people. He gives new life (John 3:3-8). His presence serves as a pledge to God's people concerning their future inheritance (Eph. 1:13-14) while enabling them to produce the fruit of salvation (Gal. 5:22-23). He is the giver of many gifts and blessings. In this chapter, we'll be looking at *justification*, the first of two important blessings.

Justification involves a change in *status*. WSC 33 provides one of the best definitions ever written.

> QUESTION: 'What is justification?'
>
> ANSWER: 'Justification is an act of God's free grace, wherein he pardons all our sins, and accepts us as righteous in his sight, only for the righteousness of Christ imputed to us and received by faith alone.'

The catechism begins by describing justification as an *act* rather than a work. It's a one-time, external action, not an ongoing, internal process. Paul makes this point in Romans 5:1: 'Therefore, since we have been justified by faith, we have peace with God through our Lord Jesus Christ'. Here the action of justification is past tense but the result is an ongoing state of peace.

Next the catechism describes justification as a removal of guilt ('pardoneth all our sins'). This means that the one-time action is a *legal* action. We're transported into a divine courtroom where God sits as judge. Charges are read and a verdict is about to be given. The first sin of the first Adam renders us guilty, so what we deserve is condemnation. But instead of receiving condemnation, the verdict is pronounced upon someone else. Our guilt is removed by the once-for-all sacrifice of the second Adam, Jesus Christ (Eph. 1:7). This has the effect of wiping the slate clean.

Justification, however, is more than a declaration of pardon. The catechism goes on to show that it's also a declaration of righteousness ('accepts us as righteous in his sight'). This is not due to our own righteousness, but 'only for the righteousness of Christ imputed to us'. It's as if we were the ones who kept the whole law perfectly and earned this righteousness. Paul expressed this as follows: 'Now to the one who works, his wages are not counted as a gift but as his due. And to the one who does not work but believes in him who justifies the ungodly, his faith is counted as righteousness' (Rom. 4:4-5). Verse 4 tells us what we already know: the worker deserves his wages. The problem is that the wages of sin is death (Rom. 6:23). Verse 5, however, teaches us something completely different: the undeserving person receives a *gift* rather than wages. This means that we get the credit for Christ's obedience. Rather than a clean slate, we now have a *full* slate of righteousness credited to our account!

So how do we receive this full slate of righteousness? The catechism states that justification is received by faith alone. It defines faith in Jesus Christ as 'a saving grace, whereby we receive and rest upon him alone for salvation, as he is offered to us in the gospel' (WSC 86).

Faith is an *instrument* – a channel for receiving God's grace, his unmerited favor towards sinners. Ephesians 2:8 teaches, 'For by grace you have been saved *through* faith. And this is not your own doing; it is the gift of God'. This is why the catechism calls faith a 'saving grace'. Some people would disagree with this notion. Faith, they would say, is something we do. This is partially true, since no one can believe for another person. But in order to exercise our faith, we need God's help. God doesn't supply the grace and we supply the faith; He supplies everything!

Faith is also a change in *perspective*. It's stepping outside of oneself and accepting the gift of another. Here the catechism speaks about *receiving*. In order to receive Jesus as He is offered in the gospel, you have to know something about Him. Paul asked, 'How are they to believe in him of whom they've never heard?' (Rom. 10:14) Good question! In order to believe in Jesus Christ, you have to know what the Bible says about Him.

Faith, however, is more than just knowing something about Jesus. Receiving Jesus means embracing what the Bible says about Jesus. John 1:12 says, 'But to all who did receive him, who believed in his name, he gave the right to become children of God'. When we receive Jesus, we become part of God's family.

Receiving is an intellectual, even emotional activity, but trusting is volitional; it involves an act of the will. The catechism refers to this activity as *resting* – not a cure for drowsiness, but a state of confidence. 'Now faith is the substance of things hoped for, the evidence of things not seen' (Heb. 11:1 KJV). This is how one Roman Centurion felt. When Jesus was willing to come to his house and heal his servant, he said, 'only say the word, and my servant will be healed'. How did Jesus respond to this astonishing statement? 'Truly I tell you, with no one in Israel have I found such faith' (Matt. 8:8, 10).

Why does the catechism insist that justification is received by faith *alone*? The reason is that it has nothing to do with works 'so no one may boast' (Eph. 2:9). Paul drove this point home in Galatians 2:16: 'Yet we know that a person is not justified by works of the law but through faith in Jesus Christ, so we also have believed in Christ Jesus, in order to be justified by faith in Christ and not by works of the law, because by works of the law no one will be justified'. How important was this to Paul? Three times he contrasted faith and works. It's as if he boldfaced, underlined, and italicized his statement! It was so important that he used the harshest language in the New Testament for those who made justification dependent upon works. He labeled such teaching as 'a different gospel' and called down curses on its supporters (Gal. 1:6-9). Clearly, the gospel leaves no room for human contribution.

So does this mean that works have no importance? On the contrary, works are important; they provide the *evidence* of faith. This was the concern of James who wrote that 'faith apart from works is useless' and 'a person is justified by works and not by faith alone' (James 2:20, 24). But doesn't this contradict what Paul wrote in Galatians? Not in the least, since James had a different focus in his letter. While Paul was combating those who wanted to include works as a condition for salvation, James was reacting against others who claimed to have faith but had nothing to show for it. He illustrated, 'If a brother or sister is poorly clothed and lacking in daily food, and one of you says to them, "Go in peace, be warmed and filled", without giving them the things needed for the body, what good is that? So also faith by itself, if it does not have works, is dead' (James 2:15-17). James was concerned about an intellectual faith that doesn't translate into action. He advocated the need for a *living* faith, one that begins in the mind but finds its way to the heart; one that's demonstrated in the Christian life.

Questions for Review and Discussion

1. Why is justification called an *act* of God's free grace?
2. On what basis does justification involve the forgiveness of sins? Explain *imputation*.

3. Explain how justification involves a declaration of righteousness.
4. Explain the parts of saving faith.
5. What is the relationship between faith and works?
6. Why do Paul and James have different things to say about justification?

Chapter 7

SPIRIT
Applying What God Is Doing

In the previous chapter, we were introduced to the work of the Holy Spirit, especially His role in applying the benefits of salvation. In justification, He unites us to Christ who earned a favorable verdict for His people. We now turn to sanctification, where He takes up residence and changes God's people from within.

Justification deals with the legal consequences of sin by removing the guilt of the sinner. What about the corruption of sin? That's the unique function of sanctification. Rather than a change in status, sanctification involves a change in *nature*. It's the work of the Spirit in us (Rom. 15:16).

Again the catechism provides us with an excellent definition in question and answer 35:

Question: 'What is sanctification?'

Answer: 'Sanctification is the work of God's free grace whereby we are renewed in the whole man after the image

> of God, and are enabled more and more to die unto sin, and live unto righteousness.'

Notice the difference between these two blessings. Justification is an *act* of God's free grace, but sanctification is a *work* – an internal and ongoing process in the life of the Christian.

Sanctification means *separation*, a setting apart for holy purposes. It starts at the beginning of the Christian life (1 Cor. 6:11; 2 Thess. 2:13) where God's people are freed from the power of sin (Rom. 6:6, 11).

That's the initial sense. The catechism, however, emphasizes the progressive sense by describing sanctification as a *renewal* of the image of God. Earlier we learned that God's moral attributes were communicated to man, His image-bearer. Man's fall into sin corrupted the image beyond recognition. Now in sanctification, the image is being renewed (Titus 3:5). Yet there's also a sense that it's being *progressively* renewed. Paul exhorted his readers 'to be renewed in the spirit of your minds, and to put on the new self, created after the likeness of God in true righteousness and holiness' (Eph. 4:23-24). Here, the moral attributes of knowledge, righteousness and holiness are being restored in the life of the Christian who is being conformed to the image of the Son (Rom. 8:29).

Renewal also implies the *removal* of pollution ('enabled more and more to die unto sin and live unto righteousness'). Those who already have been set free from sin (Rom. 6:7) are given the power to resist sin and lives holy lives unto God (Rom. 6:12-13). Sanctification reverses one of the original curses of sin. Paul wrote, 'Since we have these promises, beloved, let us cleanse ourselves from every defilement of body and spirit, bringing holiness to completion in the fear of God' (2 Cor. 7:1). This teaches us something else about sanctification: it's a blessing in which we cooperate. This is why not every Christian grows at the same pace. The Holy

Spirit is the sanctifier, but we are called to 'walk by the Spirit' (Gal. 5:16) lest we grieve the Spirit by not cooperating in our sanctification (Eph. 4:30).

Does this mean that Christians can achieve complete sanctification (sinless perfection) in this life? By no means! The Bible is crystal clear on this matter. 'Who can say, I have made my heart pure; I am clean from my sin?' (Prov. 20:9). 'Surely there is not a righteous man on earth who does good and never sins' (Eccles. 7:20). 'If we say we have no sin, we deceive ourselves and the truth is not in us' (1 John 1:8). Sanctification is never perfect in this life because Christians experience 'the remnants of sin abiding in every part of them' and the 'perpetual lustings of the flesh against the spirit' (WLC 78).

Yet the fact that 'nobody's perfect' should grieve us. We were created to be perfect! And one day we shall be. God's people will be fully sanctified at death and especially when Christ returns (1 Cor. 15:42; Phil. 3:20-21; 1 John 3:2). Until then, we must be on guard against the temptation to justify our sin or live comfortably with our transgressions.

Sanctification expresses itself in the Christian life through *obedience*. God's people respond to His grace with sincere gratitude (Ps. 130:3-4). Jesus puts it rather bluntly: 'If you love me, you will keep my commandments' (John 14:15). Which commandments? God doesn't leave us guessing about the details. His law tells us not only *whom* to obey but *what* to obey.

The Bible reveals three uses of the law. First, it maintains order in society. Since God establishes all forms of authority on earth, whoever resists authority ends up resisting God (Rom. 13:1-2). Second, the law is a schoolmaster, teaching people that they are sinners in need of a savior (Rom. 3:19-20; 7:7-8). Third, it teaches Christians to live a life of gratitude expressed in holiness (Titus 2:11-14).

While the law of gratitude shows up in various places in the Bible, it is 'summarily comprehended' in the Ten Commandments (WSC 41). This grouping found in Exodus 20 and Deuteronomy 5 provides a summary of the law. Each commandment can be considered in a positive and negative way. Each has an internal and external significance. Since space limits a full study of the Ten Commandments, the following questions and scriptural references are included for reflection and future discussion.

1. **First Commandment ('Whom we worship')**
   - What does the Bible say about atheists? (Ps. 14:1)
   - What does the Bible say about other gods and saviors? (Deut. 4:39; Ps. 96:5; John 14:6; Acts 4:12)
   - Is it okay to love something as much as God? (Matt. 6:24)
2. **Second Commandment ('How we worship')**
   - Is it proper to worship God through an image? (Exod. 20:4-6; Rom. 1:21-24)
   - Are all images unlawful? (1 Kings 6:18; Num. 21:8-9, but cf. 2 Kings 18:4)
   - Are images of Christ appropriate? (Col. 1:15; 1 Peter 1:8; 1 John 3:2)
3. **Third Commandment ('Reverence')**
   - What does God's name describe? (1 Chron. 29:10-13)
   - What were the consequences of misusing God's name? (Exod. 20:7; Lev. 24:16)
   - How does this affect the way we treat God's Word? (Ps. 138:2)

4. Fourth Commandment ('Entering God's rest')

- Why did God rest on the seventh day? (Gen. 2:2-3; Isa. 40:28; Ps. 99:1)
- Why did God command His people to rest on the seventh day? (Exod. 20:8-11; Deut. 5:15)
- What is the meaning of God's rest for His people? (Heb. 4:9-10).
- How should Christians observe this rest? (Isa. 58:13 with vv. 3-4; Heb. 10:21-25)
- What continues or discontinues from the Old Testament Sabbath to the New Testament Lord's Day? (Luke 23:56-24:1; Col. 2:16-17; Acts 20:7)

5. Fifth Commandment ('Authority')

- What is a Christian's responsibility in the home? (Exod. 20:12; Eph. 6:1-4)
- What is a Christian's responsibility in the church? (Heb. 13:17)
- What is a Christian's responsibility in society? (Rom. 13:1-2; 1 Pet. 2:13-17).

6. Sixth Commandment ('Life')

- What is the basis for this commandment? (Gen. 9:6)
- What is specifically forbidden in this commandment? (Exod. 20:13)
- When does life begin? (Luke 1:41; Ps. 139:13-16)
- Is this commandment only concerned with outward violence? (Matt. 5:21-22)

7. **Seventh Commandment ('Purity')**
   - What is the basis for this commandment? (Gen. 2:23-24; Eph. 5:25)
   - What is specifically forbidden in this commandment? (Exod. 20:14)
   - What about intimate relations outside of marriage? (Deut. 22:13-21)
   - What about homosexuality? (Lev. 18:22; Rom. 1:26-27; 1 Cor. 6:9)
   - What about divorce? (Mal. 2:16; Matt. 19:3-9; 1 Cor. 7:15).
   - Is this commandment only concerned with outward impurity? (Matt. 5:27-28)

8. **Eighth Commandment ('Stewardship')**
   - What is the basis for this commandment? (Ps. 50; Matt. 25:14-30)
   - What is specifically forbidden in this commandment? (Exod. 20:15)
   - What is the opposite of stealing? (Eph. 4:28)

9. **Ninth Commandment ('Truthfulness')**
   - What is the basis for this commandment? (Col. 3:9-10; Heb. 6:18)
   - What is specifically forbidden in this commandment? (Exod. 20:16)
   - What else is forbidden in this commandment? (Prov. 20:19)

10. Tenth Commandment ('Contentment')

- What is specifically forbidden in this commandment? (Exod. 20:17)
- How does this sin lead to other sins? (Gen. 4:1-8; Josh. 7:21)
- What is implicitly encouraged in this commandment? (Heb. 13:5)

Questions for Review and Discussion

1. Why is sanctification called a *work* of God's free grace?
2. Explain how sanctification involves renewal.
3. What role do God's people play in sanctification?
4. Can God's people achieve sinless perfection in this lifetime? Why or why not?
5. What are the three uses of the Law?
6. How should God's people interpret the Ten Commandments?

PART 2
Reformed Distinctives

INTRODUCTION

Christianity is defined by its essential teachings, but it involves *more* than essential teachings. Jesus said to His disciples, 'Go and make disciples of all nations, baptizing them in the name of the Father and of the Son and of the Holy Spirit, teaching them to observe *everything* I commanded you' (Matt. 28:19). If we are to learn everything He commanded then we need to learn more than the essentials.

While Christian essentials describe the *being* of the church, Reformed distinctives involve the *well-being* of the church. One can disagree with these teachings and still be a Christian.

Presbyterianism is the English-speaking branch of the Reformed tradition stemming from the Protestant Reformation. It has been exemplified by men like John Knox in Scotland (1514-1572), Charles Hodge in America (1797-1878), and especially, the commissioners to the Westminster Assembly which met in London at Westminster Abbey (1643-52). This tradition seeks to reform the Church more fully to the teachings of the Bible. This book presents three distinctives: TULIP, government, and worship.

Chapter 8

TULIP
Doctrines Of Grace

TULIP is an *acronym*. It's a word made up of the first letters of other words. It offers an understanding of salvation from the standpoint of God, showcasing the plan of salvation through the lens of the Trinity.

The acronym of TULIP yields the following doctrines:

1. **T**otal Depravity
2. **U**nconditional Election
3. **L**imited Atonement
4. **I**rresistible Grace
5. **P**erseverance of the Saints

Total depravity

Total depravity brings us back to the doctrine of sin. It describes the *totality* of sin, how corruption has penetrated every part of human nature. In Noah's day, it meant that 'every intention of the thoughts of man's heart was only evil continually' (Gen. 6:5). But then came the flood. Mankind was wiped out and God started over with Noah. Did this solve the problem? Not quite. For after the flood, God surveyed the condition of His image-bearers and came to the following conclusion: 'the intention of man's heart is evil from his youth' (Gen. 8:21). The flood didn't change human nature. Noah was still a descendant of Adam. He was better than the rest of his generation, but he was still an heir to that sinful legacy. He proved it by getting drunk and lying uncovered (Gen. 9:21). Paul summed it up well with these words: 'No one does good, not even one' (Rom. 3:12).

Total depravity is bad enough. This malady, however, yields something even more problematic. It leads to *total inability*. It renders man incapable of choosing God. In his epistles, Paul spoke of what is sinful and unconverted in terms of 'flesh' and 'natural man'. He admitted that 'the mind that is set on the flesh is hostile to God, for it does not submit to God's law; indeed it *cannot*' (Rom. 8:7) He acknowledged 'the natural person does not accept the things of the Spirit of God, for they are folly to him, and he is not able to understand them because they are spiritually discerned' (1 Cor. 2:14). Something is broken. Natural man doesn't reject God because he's deprived of knowledge. He rejects God because he's depraved in nature. In our natural state, it's impossible to believe in God. This is bad news.

It also raises another question: How can God call us to faith if we are incapable of believing; didn't He give us free will? The answer is that free will refers to choices determined by our nature. For example, we can choose to go swimming determined to breathe underwater, but we don't have the power to breathe water. What comes naturally to fish is impossible for mankind. It would require a change in nature. In a similar way, we do not have the power to choose God unless our nature is changed. Even God is subject to this principle. He is the freest being in the universe, but can only act according to His nature. We already learned that it's impossible for God to lie (Heb. 6:18). Since we are made in the image of God, there are things that are impossible for us too. We must act according to our nature.

Unconditional Election

If this is the case, then how can we be saved from our sins? We can't unless God takes the initiative. Paul provides us with what has come to be known as a 'golden chain of salvation' in Romans 8:29-30. The chain begins in the mind of God: 'Those he foreknew, he predestined'. Here, it's important to understand what the Bible means by foreknowledge. This is not bare knowledge or intellectual information; it always involves a *relationship*. God says to His prophet Jeremiah: 'Before I formed you in the womb, I knew you and before you were born I consecrated you; I appointed you a prophet to the nations' (Jer. 1:5). Here, knowledge is connected with entering a relationship. God doesn't simply know about us; He knows us *intimately*.

Foreknowledge is only the beginning; it leads to *predestination*. The Bible expresses this doctrine in two ways: election unto life and reprobation unto death. First God, 'out of his mere good pleasure, from all eternity, elected some to everlasting life' (WSC 20). Paul writes, 'Even as he chose us in him before the foundation of the world … In love, he predestined us for adoption as sons through Jesus Christ, according to the purpose of his will' (Eph. 1:4-5). Here we learn a number of things about election. It's *eternal*, occurring before the foundation of the world. It's *purposeful*, corresponding to God's perfect will. And last but not least, it's *loving*. In love, God predestined sinners to be adopted as His children.

While the doctrine of election is clearly taught in Ephesians chapter 1, its fullest expression is found in Romans chapter 9. Reflecting on the prophecy given to Rebekah concerning her twin sons, Paul wrote:

> Though they were not yet born and had done nothing either good or bad – in order that God's purpose in election might continue, not because of works but because of him who calls – she was told, 'The older will serve the younger'. As it is written, 'Jacob I loved, but Esau I hated' (Rom. 9:11-13).

Notice that God's choice had nothing to do with their actions. They had not yet done anything good or bad. It was not by any future works, but solely by God's call that Jacob was chosen and Esau was not. Faith follows election; no one can believe in Jesus Christ unless he has been appointed to believe in Jesus Christ (Acts 13:48).

Some would object to the fairness of this arrangement. Paul, however, anticipated this objection and answered it as follows:

> Is there injustice on God's part? By no means! For he says to Moses, 'I will have mercy on whom I have mercy, and I will have compassion on whom I have compassion'. So then it depends not on human will or exertion, but on God, who has mercy (Rom. 9:14-16).

Notice the emphasis on mercy and compassion. Rather than implying a state of innocence, this suggests a state of sin! God is under no obligation to save anyone. The fact that He saves some is an act of mercy and compassion.

But the unavoidable consequence is that He doesn't save *everyone*. Some are passed over and left in their sins. This is called *reprobation*, the second part of predestination. Without question it's a hard teaching, but still a Biblical one. Paul addresses it in the same chapter:

> For the Scripture says to Pharaoh, 'For this very purpose I have raised you up, that I might show my power in you, and that my name might be proclaimed in all the earth'. So then he has mercy on whomever he wills, and he *hardens* whomever he wills (Rom. 9:17-18).

In this context, hardening can be understood as allowing sinners to intensify their natural rebellion to God.

Jude is even more explicit: 'For certain people have crept in unnoticed who long ago were *designated* for this condemnation, ungodly people, who pervert the grace of our God into sensuality and deny our only Master and Lord, Jesus Christ' (Jude 4). Their judgment follows the same pattern as 'godless Esau' (Heb. 12:16). The hard truth is that not every name has been written in the book of life from the foundation of the world (Rev. 13:8). Only the elect can make this claim.

Unconditional election is a hard teaching, but it's given for our benefit. First, it destroys the myth of human autonomy. Natural man believes that he's doing just fine on his own, but Jesus says, 'apart from me you can do nothing' (John 15:5). Due to our total inability we can't choose God, but He can choose us. This should cause us to be humble before a sovereign God, knowing that we bring nothing to the table except our sin.

Second, the doctrine of unconditional election provides security for God's people. If election isn't based on human action, then we have nothing to fear. While faith produces works, ongoing sin compromises those works. We might go through a week feeling more like a sinner than a saint. Does this mean we are no longer children of God? Not if God chose us apart from anything we do. Having chosen us in eternity, He won't abandon us in space and time.

Limited Atonement

Foreknowledge and predestination happen in eternity, but their consequences occur in space and time. Salvation is a *Trinitarian* action. As we already have seen, God the Son entered space and time as the God-man to keep the law as the second Adam and offer Himself as a substitutionary sacrifice for the sins of His people. Now we go even deeper. The doctrine of limited atonement follows from the doctrine of unconditional election. It teaches that the Son only redeems the people whom the Father has chosen. Jesus taught this wonderful truth in the Gospel of John. In John 6:37, He explained, 'All that the Father gives me will come to me, and whoever comes to me I will never cast out'. This shows that God the Father has given His Son a people. In John 10:14-15, Jesus said, 'I am the good shepherd. I know my sheep and my sheep know me, just as the Father knows me and I know the Father; and I lay down my life for the sheep' (NIV). This develops His previous statement. Having been given a people by the Father, we now discover that Jesus will lay down His life for those people called His sheep. Finally, in John 17:9, Jesus conceded, 'I am not praying for the world but for those whom you have given me, for they are yours'. Here, Jesus made a stark contrast. He distinguished everyone else in the world from the people given to Him by the Father. Only those people are His sheep. Only those people will benefit from His sacrifice.

Despite its Biblical support, limited atonement isn't a universally accepted teaching. And to be fair, its opponents seem to have a strong Biblical case. In one of the most famous Bible verses, Jesus was given as a sacrifice because

'God so loved the world' (John 3:16). Likewise, Jesus is declared to be the propitiation for the sins of the whole world (1 John 2:2).

It's true these texts use universal language, but their precise meaning still requires interpretation. The Bible sometimes uses words like 'world' and 'all people' in a restricted sense. For example, Luke tells us a decree went out from Caesar Augustus that 'all the world should be registered' (Luke 2:1). From reading history, we know that Augustus didn't rule every nation and continent. Only the *Roman* world could receive his census. Likewise, John adopted this principle when he recorded Jesus' saying, 'And I, when I am lifted up from the earth, will draw all people to myself' (John 12:32). We know that many of His hearers didn't believe Him. Some ended up crucifying Him. One even betrayed Him. So either Jesus was wrong about drawing all people to Himself or He meant something else. Rather than intending all human beings, He was probably referring to all *sorts* of people. Gentiles as well as Jews would be drawn to Him.

So why is this doctrine so important? Because it considers the consequences of Christ's death as it relates to its effectiveness and our assurance. Some churches teach that Jesus died for everyone and therefore, everyone will be saved. This view is consistent, but unbiblical. Scripture clearly teaches that some will spend the rest of eternity under the wrath of God in hell (Matt. 10:28; Mark 9:43; Luke 13:28). Other churches teach that Jesus died for everyone but only believers will be saved. This makes faith the deciding factor in salvation. It means that Jesus didn't actually save anyone; He only provided the *possibility* of salvation for those who exercise their free will and accept the offer. The doctrine of total inability reminds us that a will oriented towards sin could never accept this offer.

Limited atonement, however, means *definite* atonement. Jesus provides more than the possibility of salvation; He actually saved His people. Elsewhere in the New Testament, John recorded the words of a praise song to Christ, 'For you were slain and by your blood you ransomed people for God from every tribe and language and people and nation' (Rev. 5:9). Here the ransoming is past tense; it already occurred in space and time. It's not a possibility that depends on human response, but an actuality based on God's plan of salvation. It means that our hope depends solely on Christ's work in history – indeed a comforting thought.

Irresistible Grace

Previously we learned that God the Spirit applies the work of Christ to His people. Now as we view the big picture, we see that the Father has chosen a people, the Son has provided salvation for that people, and now the Spirit calls that people out of their spiritual stupor and wakes them up! 'Those whom he predestined he also called' (Rom. 8:30). Or as Jesus Himself put it, 'No one can come to me unless the Father who sent me draws him' (John 6:44). No one can resist his will (Rom. 9:19).

First God issues a *general* call. This takes the form of preaching the gospel to all people. As we have seen, the doctrine of total depravity prevents people from responding on their own. The words go in one ear and out the other. As Jesus put it, 'Many are called, but few are chosen' (Matt. 22:14).

But in the process of preaching the gospel to all people, the Spirit takes what is preached and turns it into an *effectual* call for God's elect. They gain the ability to respond and receive new life. When Paul preached the gospel at a prayer service in Philippi, many heard his message and received the general call. One of those people was a woman named Lydia. When she heard the gospel, 'the Lord *opened her heart* to pay attention to what was said by Paul' (Acts 16:14). The call became effectual, the grace irresistible (Rom. 9:19). She was born again 'through the living and abiding word of God' (1 Pet. 1:23).

Towards the beginning of His ministry, Jesus was approached by an influential religious leader named Nicodemus who wanted to talk to Him in secret. Jesus told him, 'Unless one is born again he cannot see the Kingdom of God'. This left Nicodemus confused. 'How can a man be born when he is old? Can he enter a second time unto his mother's womb and be born?' Jesus then clarified His answer. 'Unless one is born of water and the Spirit, he cannot enter the kingdom of God. That which is born of flesh is flesh and that which is born of the Spirit is spirit' (John 3:3-5). In all likelihood, Jesus was reminding this Israelite scholar about a promise of new life from the Old Testament:

> I will sprinkle clean water on you, and you shall be clean from all your uncleannesses, and from all your idols I will cleanse you. And I will give you a new heart and a new spirit I will put within you. And I will remove the heart of stone from your flesh and give you a heart of flesh. And I will put my Spirit within you and cause you to walk in my statutes and be careful to obey my rules (Ezek. 36:25-27).

The doctrine of irresistible grace means God grants new life to sinners incapable of choosing God. Those whom the Father chooses the Son redeems. Those whom the Son redeems the Spirit awakens and gives new life. Those who receive the blessings of the Trinity will certainly come to saving faith in Jesus Christ.

Perseverance of the Saints

This chapter has taught us that salvation is a Trinitarian action: the Father elects, the Son redeems and the Spirit calls. Therefore it follows that the recipients of these actions cannot lose their salvation and will persevere to the end.

The Bible asserts this logic. 'Those whom he justified, he *glorified*' (Rom. 8:30). Notice that the end of Paul's chain of salvation is past tense. You may ask, 'How is this possible? We're still on earth, struggling with our sin'. From God's perspective, it's a done deal. What He starts, He finishes – or in Paul's words: 'He who began a good work in you will bring it to completion at the day of Jesus Christ' (Phil. 1:6). Our glorification will coincide with the return of Christ at the end of the age.

Some struggle with this teaching. After all, there are texts that seem to teach the opposite. Hebrews 6:4-6 is a case in point:

> For it is impossible, in the case of those who have once been enlightened, who have tasted the heavenly gift, and have shared in the Holy Spirit, and have tasted the goodness of the word of God and powers of the age to come, and have then fallen away, to restore them again to repentance since they are crucifying once again the Son of God to their own harm and holding him up to contempt.

We need to take this seriously. This is a real warning against *apostasy* – renouncing the faith. People walk away from God every day. But before we go along with this thinking, we need to ask a simple question: 'Were they really saved in the first place?' The Apostle John has this in mind when he wrote:

> They went out from us, but they were not of us; for if they had been of us, they would have continued with us. But they went out, that it might become plain that they all are not of us (1 John 2:19).

The challenge is that we don't have any divine insight into these things. Not every church member who walks away from the faith is irrevocably lost. Only God knows the heart. So when the general call is issued – when the gospel is preached to everyone – the elect will come in. Sometimes they stray for a time. Think of the Apostle Peter who denied the Lord three times in the courtyard of the High Priest (Luke 22:52-62). Was it impossible for him to be restored? By no means; the Lord Himself restored Peter. He was one of the sheep. No one was going to snatch Peter out of His hand (John 10:28).

But then there are people in our churches who seem genuine. They look the part, talk the talk, and walk the walk – at least for a while. While they stay, they may experience some blessings for a time like 'tasting the goodness of the Word of God'. And then something will happen. Maybe they'll disagree with someone in the church. Possibly the sin they're hiding will come to light. They'll end up fighting or fleeing the discipline of the church and then they'll be gone. They might end up at another church or just give up on the faith altogether. Only God knows the heart, but He has given the church a responsibility to warn apostates about the dire consequences of leaving the faith. 'They went out from us, but they were not of us.'

So perseverance means persistence. It means pressing on to the end. For Paul, it meant running a race and gaining an imperishable wreath (1 Cor. 9:24). But it's not a race that we run alone. Perseverance, you see, also means *preservation*. It means that God not only saves us, He keeps us. Paul acknowledged this wonderful truth: 'Not that I have already obtained this or am already perfect, but I press on to make it my own, because Christ Jesus has made me his own' (Phil. 3:12). May we do likewise, God helping us.

Questions for Review and Discussion

1. What does total depravity mean? Why didn't the Flood take care of the problem?
2. What does total inability mean?
3. How does man have free will?
4. What is involved in foreknowledge?
5. Explain the two parts of predestination. Why are some people offended by the doctrine of predestination?
6. What is limited atonement and how does it logically follow from unconditional election?
7. Why is limited atonement important?
8. What is irresistible grace and how does it logically follow from limited atonement?
9. What is the difference between general and effectual calling? What happens in the latter?
10. What is perseverance of the saints and how does it logically follow from the rest of TULIP?

CHAPTER 9

GOVERNMENT
Biblically Balanced

Churches are not just the sum total of believers and their families; they are organizations with intentional structures. Not every church member has the same role in the overall structure. Some teach, others rule without teaching, still others serve without ruling. Is government good for the church? God thinks so. He desires that church affairs be done 'properly and in an orderly manner' (1 Cor. 14:40 NASB). The Bible speaks about church government, not in detailed form, but sufficiently for God's people to know how to organize as His church.

Foundations

Before we consider specifics, it's important to understand the foundations of church government. Earlier we learned that man was created to rule the lesser creation. Even after man's fall into sin, God appointed rulers to govern His world. This also applied to Israel, His chosen nation. He appointed Moses as lawgiver, Samuel as judge, and David as king.

Even after the nation was conquered and sent into exile, God returned His people to the land under the leadership of Ezra the priest and Nehemiah the governor.

Old Testament Israel was not an end in itself. It was a kingdom that needed to be expanded. In the New Testament, the Israel of old was broadened to become the 'Israel of God' (Gal. 6:16), a commonwealth that included both Jews and Gentiles (Eph. 2:11-22). This is called the church of Jesus Christ. Like the Israel of Old, the church is called a holy nation (Exod. 19:6; 1 Pet. 2:9) and a visible manifestation of the kingdom of God on earth (Rev. 1:4-6).

Every kingdom requires a king. The rulers of Old Testament Israel served as types and shadows of the ultimate ruler of God's people. In Matthew 28:18, Jesus spoke these words to His church: 'All authority in heaven and on earth has been given to me'. Here stood a lawgiver greater than Moses, a judge greater than Samuel, and the King greater than David.

Like His Father who ruled through His image bearers, Jesus rules through His office-bearers. To His immediate successors He said, 'I assign to you, as my Father assigned to me, a kingdom' (Luke 22:29). How should they exercise this authority? Jesus told them, 'I will give you the keys of the kingdom of heaven, and whatever you bind on earth shall be bound in heaven, and whatever you loose on earth shall be loosed in heaven' (Matt. 16:19; 18:18). This is legal language. Binding involves closing, while loosing involves opening. Binding declares that someone is outside of the Church through unbelief or censure while loosing proclaims that a person is loosed from sin and received into the Church.

Notice that Jesus didn't give this power to everyone. He gave it to the apostles. But these elite disciples aren't around anymore. They served as a foundational level of leadership by receiving and recording the word of God (Eph. 2:20). The leadership passed from them to others called *presbyters*. In Acts chapter 20, Paul instructed the Ephesian presbyters (v. 17) to rule the church to which the Holy Spirit made them overseers (v. 28). The office of presbyter continues to govern the church today.

Presbyterian Government

Different churches have different forms of government. Some are hierarchical with ranking officials both inside and outside the local church while others resist outside influence. The former is called *Episcopalianism* while the latter is known as *Congregationalism*. Neither best expresses the form of Biblical government.

Episcopalianism is defined as a church ruled by *bishops*. The word stems from the Greek word *episkopos* which means 'bishop' or 'overseer'. It's a hierarchical system with early roots in church history. At the top sits the archbishop, or in the case of Roman Catholicism, the pope. While Episcopalianism has some attractive features such as a clearly defined chain-of-command and an impressive historical pedigree, it lacks Biblical support. Scripture, you see, links a bishop (*episkopos*) with a presbyter (*presbuteros*). We've already seen that the Ephesian presbyters were considered to be overseers/bishops of the church. In Titus chapter 1, the appointed presbyters (v. 5) were also called to be overseers/bishops (v. 7). Church tradition, however ancient and efficient, must always submit to the greater authority of Biblical revelation.

Congregationalism or independency is defined as a church ruled by the *congregation*. This is the system employed by most evangelical churches today. While this system recognizes different offices within the local church, it resists hierarchies and generally de-emphasizes connections with other churches. In such a system, inter-church connections, however useful, are still optional. Accountability outside of the congregation is a matter of preference.

The Bible, however, presents the church as interconnected. Acts 15:1-30 describes the meeting of the Jerusalem Council that was convened to deal with the heresy of the Judaizers – those who wanted to impose the Mosaic Law as a condition for salvation. This Council included commissioners from different churches. In fact, Paul, Barnabas, and some others were appointed to attend this counsel on behalf of the churches in Asia Minor. When they arrived in Jerusalem, they were welcomed by the church collective (vv. 2-4). Then the council debated the issue (v. 7), came to an agreement (vv. 19-21), and implemented their decision through a circular letter (vv. 22-30). This council ruled on a vital doctrinal matter that affected the whole church. If it had only been a voluntary meeting, then heresy could have been tolerated in some local or regional churches. Permitting but not requiring broader assemblies has the potential to compromise the broader accountability of the church.

What is the alternative to these inadequate forms of church government? The answer is *Presbyterianism*. This is defined as a church ruled by presbyters at local, regional, and denominational levels. Presbyter comes from the Greek *presbuteros* which means 'older' or 'elder'. In Biblical times, older men had the respect and maturity to lead their families and communities. These 'elders' served as representatives of the people in covenant dealings (Exod. 24:9; 2 Sam. 5:3; 1 Kings 8:1) and exercised authority over Israel (Deut. 19:12; Josh. 20:4). Yet over time, this term became more flexible. It could describe rulers distinguished from priests or scribes (Luke 20:1), an assembly of rulers that included priests and scribes (Acts 4:8), or a tradition of scribes (Matt. 15:2). Presbyters were present in the synagogue (Luke 7:3-5) and in the earliest congregations of the church (Acts 11:30; 14:23).

With all of these possibilities, how should we interpret this word? The answer is found in 1 Timothy 5:17: 'Let the elders who rule well be considered worthy of a double honor, especially those who labor in preaching and teaching'. Here we see the flexibility of the term in allowing for two groups under the same heading. The former group could be older men who rule their house well (1 Tim. 5:1) or officers who rule the church well (Rom. 12:8; 1 Cor. 12:28). The latter group, however, are singled out for a specific reason: they labored in preaching and teaching. The New Testament uses different titles to describe this group. As servants of the word, they are called *ministers* (Luke 1:2; Eph. 6:21), in respect to oversight, they are known as *overseers* (Phil. 1:1; 1 Tim. 3:1), as shepherds of the flock, they are considered *pastors* (Eph. 4:11; 1 Pet. 5:2), as instructors of the faith, they are designated *teachers* (1 Cor. 12:28-29; Eph. 4:11), and for the respect of the office, they are deemed *presbyters* (Acts 20:17; Titus 1:5-8; 1 Pet. 5:1). Like the New Testament elders who succeed their Old Testament counterparts, these New Testament word-ministers succeed the *prophets* who proclaimed God's word to His people (Isa. 52:7/Rom. 10:15; Col. 1:25-28; 2 Tim. 4:2, 5) and the *priests* who publicly taught the word (Deut. 31:9-11; 2 Chron. 15:3; Neh. 8:1-9) and administered the sacraments (Lev. 6:8-30; Heb. 9:1-10). Word ministers are set apart as officers in the church by their gifts and calling.

Presbyterianism involves more than local presbyters. It's also expressed by the word *presbuterion* (presbytery). Paul wrote to Timothy, 'Do not neglect the gift you have, which was given you by prophecy when the *presbytery* laid their hands on you' (1 Tim. 4:14). Here the presbytery recognized Timothy's gift and ordained him to use it. The Council of Jerusalem was composed of apostles and presbyters (Acts 15:4). This means that presbyters function at various levels. Presbyterian churches are interconnected from the session (local government) to the presbytery (regional government) to the general assembly (denomination-level government).

There is also a third office in Presbyterian government. The Bible speaks of the office of deacon (*diaconos,* a word that can also means *minister* or more commonly, *servant*) which assists the church by attending to the temporal needs of the people. The first deacons assisted the apostles by 'serving tables', freeing them up to focus on word-ministry and prayer (Acts 6:1-7). Later deacons also assisted presbyters (1 Tim. 3:8-13), a practice that continues into the present. Through these offices and their interconnections at various levels, Presbyterianism provides a Biblically-balanced approach to church government.

Questions for Review and Discussion

1. What are the Old Testament foundations for church government and how did they find fulfillment in the New Testament?
2. How does Christ rule His Church?
3. What is Episcopalianism and what are its problems?
4. What is congregationalism and what are its problems?
5. What is Presbyterianism? How does the Old Testament inform our understanding of this system?
6. How are word ministers and ruling elders differentiated in the New Testament?
7. What are the origins and responsibilities of deacons?

Chapter **10**

WORSHIP
According To Scripture

There's a war going on. It's not a war on foreign soil, but right here in this country. It's not war in the conventional sense, but a *worship* war. On one side there are the traditionalists with their organs, hymnals, and nostalgia. On the other side, there are the progressives with their screens, praise choruses, and excitement. So who is right? Too often the answer depends on the feelings or tastes of the participants. Such answers focus on the worshiper rather than God who is the object of worship. The right answer, however, depends on what God defines as worship.

The Regulative Principle

People approach worship in different ways. Some believe that tradition should govern what is done in worship. They might appeal to the decree of a church council or the antiquity of a particular liturgy. Such *holy tradition* has ancient roots in the history of church. A noteworthy example was the decision of the Seventh Ecumenical Council (A.D. 787) to legalize the veneration of icons (images of Christ, Mary, and the saints). Even though Scripture does not warrant the use of such images, it became part of the tradition of the church. In order to be a legitimate standard, tradition must conform to the ultimate standard of Biblical revelation. When it fails to do so and is elevated to the level of Scripture, it becomes a form of idolatry. Presbyterian churches aren't immune to this tendency. If the answer to a liturgical question is 'we've always done it that way', then we have fallen into a form of holy tradition.

Most Protestant churches would not admit to practicing holy tradition; rather they would appeal to a different sort of principle. In regard to worship, they would claim that whatever is not forbidden is permissible. This is known as the *normative principle of worship*. At first glance, it seems like a reasonable principle. It accommodates the highest forms of traditionalism and the most progressive forms of contemporary worship.

The normative principle may seem reasonable, but is it truly a Biblical principle? The answer is no. God does not simply allow His people to worship Him in any way not forbidden; rather He commands us to worship according to His word. We must do whatever God directs us to do by command or implication. This is known as the *regulative principle of worship*.

Why is there a need for such a strict principle? It begins with the distinction between God and His creatures. Paul asked his readers a rhetorical question: 'Who has known the mind of the Lord or who has been His counselor?' (Rom. 11:34) The answer, of course, is *no one*. The reason for this answer is that a creature cannot know the mind of its creator apart from revelation. So if this is the case, then how can a creature properly worship its creator apart from such revelation? The answer is he cannot.

There's also a reason why he *should* not. Man is not only a creature; he is also a sinner. Ecclesiastes 9:3 has a low opinion of human inventiveness: 'the hearts of the children of man are full of evil, and madness is in their hearts while they live, and after that they go to the dead'. So if our hearts are depraved then how can we rightly decide to worship God on our own? The answer is that we cannot, and the result is idolatry. Consider how the Lord cautioned His people in Deuteronomy 4:15-18:

> Therefore watch yourselves very carefully. Since you saw no form on the day that the LORD spoke to you at Horeb out of the midst of the fire, beware lest you act corruptly by making a carved image for yourselves, in the form of any figure, the likeness of male or female, the likeness of any animal that is on the earth, the likeness of any winged bird that flies in the air, the likeness of anything that creeps on the ground, the likeness of any fish that is in the water under the earth.

And yet this is the path that Israel chose. Whether it involved golden calves (Exod. 32:4; 1 Kings 12:28) or a bronze serpent (2 Kings 18:4), God's people acted corruptly by worshiping God according to their imaginations instead of His word. In doing so they became no better than pagans, confusing the Creator with His creatures (Rom. 1:21-23).

So as a creature and a sinner, man is already handicapped when it comes to worshiping God. The Lord, however, does not leave these matters up to chance. In Deuteronomy 12:32, He declared, 'Everything that I command you, you shall be careful to do. You shall not add to it or take from it'. It goes without saying that 'everything' includes worship. Verse 31 specifically condemned the worship practices of the Canaanite nations that Israel was about to invade and dispossess.

Some may wonder if this strictness continues in the New Testament where believers are under the new (and more gracious) covenant. We are, but we still worship the same holy God. As the writer of Hebrews said, 'Let us offer to God acceptable worship, with reverence and awe, for our God is a consuming fire' (Heb. 12:28-29). God was a consuming fire in the Old Testament. The context of Hebrews 12 suggests Mount Sinai, but there is another place where God *literally* was a consuming fire. In Leviticus 10:1-4, the priests Nadab and Abihu offered unauthorized fire before the Lord. They did not worship God as He commanded and the consequence was their death; fire came out from before the Lord and consumed them. While this was an extraordinary judgment, it still shows the seriousness of worship.

Having said that the regulative principle continues from Old Testament to New Testament doesn't mean there isn't any discontinuity. It's also important to recognize the differences in worship introduced with the coming of Christ. As part of his history lesson on worship, Jesus declared to the Samaritan woman:

> The hour is coming when neither on this mountain nor in Jerusalem will you worship the Father. You worship what you do not know; we worship what we know, for salvation is from the Jews. But the hour is coming and is now here when the true worshipers will worship the Father in spirit and truth, for the Father is seeking such people to worship him. God is spirit and those who worship him must worship in spirit and truth (John 4:21-24).

This brief history lesson revealed two things. First it revealed that the Samaritans didn't worship God properly.

They refused to follow His word which is truth (John 17:17). Second it showed that Israel did worship God correctly, but not *ultimately*. Their temple worship found its fulfillment in the person and work of Jesus Christ. Here 'spirit' is equated with *fulfillment*.

What does this mean for us? It means that our worship must be sensitive to Biblical time. The Spirit describes the movement away from Old Testament types and shadows to the New Testament fulfillment in Christ. Paul warned, 'Therefore, let no one pass judgment on you in questions of food and drink, or with regard to a festival or a new moon or a Sabbath. These are a shadow of the things to come, but the substance belongs to Christ' (Col. 2:16-17). Liturgical calendars, elaborate ritual, and emphasis on sacred place reflect old covenant tendencies. On the other hand, new covenant worship stresses the fulfillment of type and shadows.

The regulative principle also serves another function: it protects the Christian's *liberty of conscience*. Since God is Lord of the conscience, Christians are bound to worship God only according to His word (WCF 20:2). Some churches introduce practices in an attempt to enhance the worship of God. In Paul's day, these took on the form of Old Testament ceremonies and harsh exercises of self-denial. While these were well-intended practices, the apostle referred to them as 'self-made religion' (Col. 2:23). Today, unbiblical forms of worship are introduced for the best of reasons. Christians have a right to oppose such practices by appealing to requirements of Scripture over the doctrines of men.

What then does Scripture require? It requires *elements* – things that must be done in worship. These include the public reading of Scripture (Neh. 8:1-8; 1 Tim. 4:13), preaching (1 Tim. 4:13; 2 Tim. 4:2), the sacraments of baptism

(Acts 2:41; 1 Cor. 1:17) and the Lord's Supper (Acts 2:42; 20:7; 1 Cor. 11:20), public prayer (Acts 2:42; 1 Tim. 2:1-3), congregational singing (Eph. 5:19; Col. 3:16), offerings (Ps. 96:8; 1 Cor. 16:1-2), and occasional vows (Rom. 10:9-13; 1 Tim. 6:12).

Notice that these are general categories. These elements can be expressed in a number of ways which we call *forms*. For example, public reading of the Scriptures involves a choice of translation. Baptism can be expressed through sprinkling, pouring, or immersion into water. The Lord's Supper involves using leavened or unleavened bread and wine or grape juice. Congregational singing might include the use of books or screens that contain renditions of psalms, hymns, or praise choruses. While the Bible gives us some latitude, we shouldn't think that every form is equally appropriate. The forms we choose may say a lot about the doctrines we believe.

There are also situations and factors that facilitate worship. According to WCF 1.6, these *circumstances* 'are to be ordered by the light of nature and Christian prudence, according to the general rules of the Word'. These might include the time and place of worship, the use of amplifying devices, and the accompaniment of musical instruments. They require the exercise of Biblical wisdom.

The Dialogical Principle

How do all the elements fit together? Is it simply a matter of personal taste? These questions can be answered by introducing another principle. It's a subtle principle, one that is sensitive to the covenantal nature of worship. We call it the *dialogical principle of worship* because it showcases the Biblical conversation between God speaking and His people responding.

In the Old Testament, this pattern was expressed in the dedication of the Temple (2 Chron. 5–7). Here the worship moved from a call to worship (5:2-5) to a sin offering that allowed for entrance into the presence of God (5:6-10). Then the worship continued with a hymn of praise (5:11-14), a sermon of sorts (6:1-11), a prayer of dedication (6:12-42), God's acceptance of the sacrifice and filling His Temple with glory (7:1-2), and congregational praise and thanksgiving (7:3).

While some may point out that 2 Chronicles chapters 5-7 is an example of a non-repeatable event in the history of salvation, a similar pattern is also found in the New Testament. We find an echo of 2 Chronicles in the heavenly worship of Revelation chapters 4-5. Here, the participants assemble (4:1-7) and sing a hymn (4:8-11). Worship, however, cannot continue without a sacrifice (5:1-5), so a sin offering is made (5:6). This, by the way, is no ordinary offering, but the Lamb who was slain – the fulfillment of all the Old Testament sacrifices! How do the people respond? They sing another hymn (5:9-10).

This is important because Revelation chapters four and five serve as a pattern for our worship. Hebrews 12:18-28 contrasts the meeting at Sinai – another dialogical encounter between God and His people – with attendance at corporate worship. Verses 18-21 recall the terror of the former encounter while verses 22-28 present the joyful (and solemn) nature of the latter. It's worth noting that both gatherings have heavenly components. The writer of Hebrews informs us that when we gather for corporate worship, we come to 'Mount Zion and to the city of the living God, the heavenly Jerusalem'. Our coming is not in a physical sense, but spiritually gathering with 'innumerable angels, the assembly of the firstborn who are enrolled in heaven, the spirits of the righteous made perfect'. Indeed, by the power of the Holy Spirit we come into the presence of God the Father through Jesus, 'the mediator of a new covenant'.

This should cause us to reflect on our attitude towards corporate worship. It's not merely a feel-good gathering that takes place in a specific location. Rather, it's a meeting of heaven and earth! It's not only a meeting of the *church militant*, struggling with the world, the flesh and the devil, but it includes the *church triumphant* who have conquered such forces and are seated in the heavenly realms. It also speaks about the nature of our God who not only saved us, but who is uniquely present with us in corporate worship. If Biblical worship follows the pattern of a dialogue, then our worship also should reflect this principle. A sample liturgy reflecting the regulative and dialogical principles is found in Appendix II.

Questions for Review and Discussion

1. What is holy tradition and how does it affect worship?
2. What is the normative principle of worship?
3. What is the regulative principle of worship? What are some reasons for this principle?
4. What are the elements of Biblical worship?
5. What are some forms of these elements?
6. What are some circumstances in worship?
7. What is the dialogical principle of worship? Give some examples from the Old and New Testaments.

PART 3
Means Of Grace

INTRODUCTION

Christianity is not a collection of individuals, but a religion of *community*. The name of that community is the church of Jesus Christ. The Bible expresses this notion in the various ways it describes the church. It is referred to as a household of God (Eph. 2:19), holy nation (1 Pet. 2:9), Israel of God (Gal. 6:16), and visible form of the kingdom of God (Matt. 16:18-19; Rev. 1:4-6).

If these titles underscore the importance of Church as a community, then we should expect to receive God's blessings when we come together as His people. God blesses His people every day of their lives, but He blesses them in a unique way through the means that are uniquely available in His church. These are called the *means of grace*.

Why does God work through means? Can't He accomplish everything by Himself? He can. After all, He created the universe out of nothing. And yet, He *chooses* to use means. Just as He ordinarily provides healing through the means of a doctor, so He ordinarily provides the benefits of salvation through the means of grace: word, sacrament, and prayer.

CHAPTER 11

PREACHING AND SACRAMENTS
The Primary Means

Preaching

We've already learned that faith comes from God (Eph. 2:8). But at the end of Romans 10, Paul explained how we receive this faith:

> How then will they call on him in whom they have not believed? And how are they to believe in him of whom they have never heard? And how are they to hear without someone preaching? And how are they to preach unless they are sent? As it is written, 'How beautiful are the feet of those who preach the good news!' ... So faith comes from hearing, and hearing through the word of Christ (Rom. 10:14-17).

Here Paul worked backwards with a series of rhetorical questions. He began by stating the obvious, namely that calling on God for salvation requires believing the gospel of salvation. Yet he didn't stop there. He went on to show that believing the gospel originates in hearing the gospel.

But is hearing really necessary? What about *reading*? After all, Paul was writing in an oral culture in the first century. And besides, the canon wasn't even closed yet! These days, enough Bibles are available for people to believe by reading the gospel for themselves. But notice that Paul didn't link hearing to reading. He linked hearing to *preaching*. And he had a specific sort of preacher in mind: those who are *sent*. It's not enough to have the ability or conviction to preach; one must also have the *authority* to preach. Such a preacher doesn't select himself; rather he must be appointed or sent by God through the agency of the church. Paul was commissioned to be an apostle by the risen Christ (Acts 26:12-18), but his disciple Timothy was ordained by the presbytery to be an evangelist (2 Tim. 4:5, 14). In the end, all of these rhetorical questions led Paul to an inevitable conclusion: faith ordinarily comes through the preaching of the gospel. Thus preaching is the primary means of grace for creating faith in the heart of a person and strengthening that faith (Rom. 16:25).

What is preaching? It's an important question for churches to consider as they offer this means of grace to their people. It's a question that involves many aspects but only one answer. Preaching involves public speaking, but is more than bare rhetoric. Preaching includes the communication of facts, but is not a lecture. Preaching concerns the changing of attitudes, but is not a motivational speech. Preaching involves all of these aspects, but is more than the sum total of them.

So what then is preaching? Preaching is *proclamation*. It's declaring Christ and all of His benefits. It's an urgent plea for sinners to understand their nature, receive God's gift of salvation, and be transformed by that gift. For the one who preaches (*kerusso*) is a herald (*kerux*) – two Greek words that are related to each other. Heralds proclaim royal messages. Romans 10:15 refers to Isaiah 52:7, a longer passage that speaks to this activity: 'How beautiful upon the mountains are the feet of him who brings good news, who publishes peace, who brings good news of happiness, who publishes salvation, who says to Zion, "Your God reigns".' Herald-preachers need to proclaim the royal message from the Bible, explaining the King's message and applying it to His subjects.

Not everyone appreciates this understanding of preaching. Many want the message to correspond to other messages that they're accustomed to hearing. They want preaching to be 'relevant' as the culture defines relevance. Paul also fought against this misconception in his day. In his first letter to the Corinthians, he contrasted the kind of preaching that the world desires with the kind that God requires:

> Jews demand signs and Greeks seek wisdom, but we preach Christ crucified, a stumbling block to Jews and folly to Gentiles, but to those who are called, both Jews and Greeks, Christ the power of God and the wisdom of God. For the foolishness of God is wiser than men, and the weakness of God is stronger than men (1 Cor. 1:22-25).

Here, the apostle divided the world into two camps. On the one hand, there were the Jews, Paul's own people, who expected preaching to include the miraculous signs and earthly hope of a restored kingdom under the rule of David's descendant. On the other hand, there were the Gentiles of the Greco-Roman world. This group was weaned on the wisdom of their culture that was at odds with Biblical revelation. The cross was a stumbling block to both groups. It meant defeat for the Jews and absurdity for the Greeks.

Today the camps have different players but similar motives. Some view religion in terms of victory over their political/cultural enemies while others find the whole enterprise irrelevant to their daily concerns. The word of God, however weak and foolish it may appear, remains the power and wisdom of God. The herald-preachers of Christ continue to be its primary channel for the modern world.

Sacraments

Preaching is not the only means of grace. God also provides visible helps called *sacraments*. Some Christians are put off by this word because it reminds them of something magical or superstitious. The word, however, comes from a Latin term that translated the New Testament Greek word for *mystery*. Paul, speaking as a word-minister, wrote, 'This is how one should regard us, as servants of Christ and stewards of the mysteries of God' (1 Cor. 4:1). Here the mystery certainly involves the stewardship of the gospel. Yet Paul spoke of mysteries *plural*. This could include the gospel in all of its forms, audible or visual.

WSC 92 defines a sacrament as 'a holy ordinance instituted by Christ, wherein, by sensible signs, Christ, and the benefits of the new covenant, are represented, sealed, and applied to believers'. First, sacraments are said to be holy ordinances. This means that they are set apart from their common use for God's special purposes. Second, they are instituted by Christ. While it can be said that Christ as the living Word of God instituted many sacraments in the Old Testament (e.g., circumcision, sacrificial system), He especially instituted two sacraments in the New Testament. These are baptism and the Lord's Supper, the subjects of the next two chapters.

The catechism calls sacraments 'sensible', not because they make sense, but because they're *sensory*. God not only provides the gospel through the audible preaching of His word, but also through other sensory means. He caters not only to our sinfulness, but also to our 'creatureliness'. Such means can be seen, smelled, touched, and tasted, so that in every way we are reminded of our spiritual benefits.

Besides being sensible, sacraments are called *signs*. Signs represent. They are pictures that describe the realities they convey. In this way they appeal to our eyes. Yet sacraments are more than signs; they are also *seals*. They confirm the realities they represent. They assure us of God's grace. Paul reminded us that '[Abraham] received the *sign* of circumcision as a *seal* of the righteousness that he had by faith while he was still uncircumcised' (Rom. 4:11).

As signs and seals, the sacraments function as means of grace. This is what the catechism means by 'applied'. There is a spiritual connection between the form the sacrament takes and the reality behind it. This is called the *sacramental union*. How close is the connection between sign and reality? This will be discussed in the course of our study.

Finally, sacraments are for *believers*. Receiving them requires faith. WSC 91 explains why this is important:

> The sacraments become effectual means of salvation, not from any virtue in them, or in him that doth administer them; but only by the blessing of Christ, and the working of his Spirit in them that by faith receive them.

Apart from faith, the water of baptism only removes dirt from the body (1 Pet. 3:21). Apart from believing, the bread and wine of communion only offer food and drink for the mouth. But when these sensible signs and seals are received by faith, they become connected to the spiritual realities. Only then do the sacraments become effectual means of salvation.

Questions for Review and Discussion

1. How do people ordinarily come to faith? How is this explained in Romans Chapter 10?
2. What are some things that people mistake for preaching?
3. What best describes preaching? Consequently, what is the function of a preacher?
4. What are some worldly preferences for preaching? What was Paul's response?
5. What's the difference between a sign and a seal?
6. What is the sacramental union?
7. How do the sacraments become effectual means of salvation?

Chapter **12**

BAPTISM
The Gracious Entrance

The sacrament of baptism has a variety of meanings. Over the course of church history, its complexities have led to a host of misunderstandings. This chapter strives to shed some light on the confusion by examining the Biblical data under three different headings: purification, initiation, and recipients.

Purification

Purification involves *washing*. We wash our hands in order to make them clean. Likewise, God provided a physical way for His people to be ceremonially clean in His presence. In the Old Testament, He commanded the priests to wash before entering the Tabernacle and Temple (Exod. 30:17-21; 2 Chron. 4:6). He directed the Levites to be sprinkled with the 'water of purification' (Num. 8:5-7). He incorporated the use of water into cleansing His people from leprosy, bodily discharges, and other diseases (Lev. 14–15). Hebrews 9:10

referred to these as 'various washings' but the Greek literally calls them 'baptisms' (*baptismois*). While some Christians argue that the word for baptism necessarily means 'immersion', this New Testament text uses it in a broader sense to describe ritual purification.

Sometimes purification was used in connection with rebirth. Ezekiel wrote his prophecy during the exile when the temple with its system of purification was destroyed. In surveying Israel's sins and uttering a prophecy of hope, the prophet wrote, 'I will sprinkle clean water on you, and you shall be clean from all your uncleanness, and from all your idols I will cleanse you. And I will give you a new heart and a new spirit I will put within you' (Ezek. 36:25-26). Here the existing vocabulary of sprinkling is coupled with the language of 'new heart/spirit' to show the newness of the purified reality that would apply to God's people in the future.

Earlier we saw how Nicodemus was confused about the need to be baptized with water and the Spirit. Jesus admonished him about his ignorance (John 3:10). A teacher of Israel should understand such things because they were foretold in the Old Testament, especially in Ezekiel 36:25-26. A teacher of Israel should have understood the connection between the sign of water and the reality of new life through purification. Paul referred to this as 'the washing of regeneration and renewal of the Holy Spirit' (Titus 3:5). Similarly, the writer of Hebrews urged his readers, 'let us draw near with a true heart in full assurance of faith, with our hearts sprinkled clean from an evil conscience and our bodies washed with pure water' (Heb. 10:22).

The purpose of washing was for God's people to remove their 'evil' from before His eyes (Isaiah 1:16). This aspect of purification focuses on the need for *repentance* – turning away from sin. In the New Testament, John's baptism was called 'a baptism of repentance for the forgiveness of sins' (Luke 3:3). It was administered to Israel in preparation for the coming Messiah. Not surprisingly, Christian baptism is also accompanied by repentance. In his Pentecost sermon, the Apostle Peter declared, 'Repent and be baptized every one of you in the name of Jesus Christ for the forgiveness of your sins, and you will receive the gift of the Holy Spirit' (Acts 2:38).

This raises a question: 'Does baptism actually cause the forgiveness of sins?' The answer is that it doesn't cause forgiveness but is closely associated with it. This is evidenced in other places in the Book of Acts. In the next chapter, Peter declared to his hearers, 'Repent, therefore, and turn back, that your sins may be blotted out' (Acts 3:19). Here, repentance without baptism is expressed as the means of receiving forgiveness. Further along, a certain jailor from Philippi asked the Apostle Paul a very important question: 'What must I do to be saved?' What was Paul's answer? 'Believe in the Lord Jesus, and you will be saved, you and your household' (Acts 16:30-31). Faith, the flipside of repentance, was the instrument of salvation for the jailor and his family. Baptism then followed faith, not as an instrument but as a sacrament (Acts 16:32-33).

Initiation

Besides purification, Christian baptism also serves as a sacrament of *initiation* – inclusion in the covenant and admission into the visible church. The Lord expressed this to Abraham through the giving of its Old Testament counterpart, circumcision: 'This is my covenant which you shall keep, between me and you and your offspring after you: Every male among you shall be circumcised.

You shall be circumcised in the flesh of your foreskins and it shall be a sign of the covenant between me and you' (Gen. 17:10-11). Circumcision became the sign and seal of entering into God's covenant community, with God separating His people from the world and calling them to a life of holiness. Here, the outward sign corresponded to the inward reality of regeneration called the 'circumcision of the heart' (Deut. 30:6; Jer. 4:4; Rom. 2:28-29). The sign, however, emphasized curse as well as blessing. Just as the foreskin was being cut off so also would the recipient be *fully* cut off if he does not keep the rules of the covenant (see Exod. 4:25). Therefore, the reality of circumcision was two-fold. It signified and sealed new life or an untimely death.

The circumcised community, however, was intended to be a 'light to the Gentiles' (Isa. 49:6). They failed in this mission. Rather than evidencing the light, they chased after the darkness. Even though their flesh was circumcised, their hearts were uncircumcised (Jer. 9:25). By the first century A.D., circumcision had become associated with cultural Judaism. Christ, however, accomplished what Israel failed to do; His light brought the uncircumcised Gentiles into the house of God (Eph. 2:11-22). Consequently, there is no longer any distinction between Jew and Gentile (Gal. 3:28), for both the physically circumcised and uncircumcised are justified by faith in Jesus Christ (Rom. 3:30).

His accomplishment also fulfilled the Old Testament sacrament of circumcision. Paul wrote, 'In him also you were circumcised with a circumcision made without hands, by putting off the body of the flesh, by the circumcision of Christ' (Col. 2:11). In this text, the apostle was describing a different circumcision than the cutting ritual of the Old Testament. First, it involved the union of Christ with His people ('in him'). He undertook the work of redemption as their federal head, and they were included in Him. Second, this circumcision was performed 'without hands'. Here, Mark 14:58 contributes to our understanding: 'I will destroy this temple that is made with hands, and in three days I will build another, not made with hands'. The gospel writer was contrasting a man-made physical structure ('this temple made with hands') with one that God Himself constructed, namely Christ's resurrected body ('another not made with hands'). In a similar way, the physical circumcision done by man is contrasted with the circumcision that was done by God Himself. This circumcision, however, was not the sealing of new life, but an untimely death! It was the ultimate 'putting off the body of the flesh' – the full cutting off of Christ on the cross in the place of His covenant-breaking people (Col. 1:22).

What does this have to do with baptism? Paul continued from verse 11: 'having been buried with him in baptism, in which you were also raised with him through faith in the powerful working of God, who raised him from the dead' (Col. 2:12). In this passage, circumcision ('in him you were circumcised') corresponds to baptism ('having been buried with him in baptism'). The former points forward and the latter backward to the cross ('the circumcision of Christ'). This is supported elsewhere, when Jesus lamented, 'I have a baptism to be baptized with, and how great is my distress until it is accomplished!' (Luke 12:50).

Since Christians live on the other side of the cross, there is no longer any need for circumcision. Baptism has replaced the old sacrament as the sign and seal of covenant inclusion. This is why Jesus commanded His disciples, 'Go therefore and make disciples of all nations, baptizing them in the name of the Father and of the Son and of the Holy Spirit' (Matt. 28:19). God's name is being written upon them in water as a mark of ownership. Like circumcision of old, baptism involves an outward sign coupled to the inward reality of inclusion among God's people (1 Cor. 12:13).

Recipients

Understanding the nature of baptism leads to a natural question: who should be baptized? Is this sacrament only for mature individuals who personally confess Christ? This is the common answer; most Bible-believing churches hold to this view. They also seem to have some Biblical support. In the New Testament, there are examples of people first coming to faith and then submitting to baptism. Yet baptism in the New Testament doesn't only happen to believers. It happens to families and households. And this shouldn't surprise us; God has always dealt with His people in this way. The following six arguments support the claim that baptism is for believers and their children.

1. In the Old Testament, God made His covenant with Abraham and his children through circumcision. Abraham believed before he was circumcised (Rom. 4:9-11), but his children were circumcised before they believed (Gen. 17:10-13).

2. In the old covenant, God's promises involved believers and their children. 'And as for me, this is my covenant with them,' says the LORD: 'My Spirit that is upon you, and my words that I have put in your mouth, shall not depart out of your mouth, or out of the mouth of your offspring, or out of the mouth of your children's offspring,' says the LORD, 'from this time forth and forevermore' (Isa. 59:21). As it turns out, the New Covenant uses similar language. 'And Peter said to them, "Repent and be baptized every one of you in the name of Jesus Christ for the forgiveness of your sins, and you will receive the gift of the Holy Spirit. For the promise is for you and for your children and for all who are far off, everyone

whom the Lord our God calls to himself"' (Acts 2:38-39). The latter passage not only shows continuity, but expands upon the former to show the inclusion of the Gentiles ('for all who are far off').

Admittedly it's true that New Testament baptism was often preceded by faith. After all, it occurred in the context of missions where pagans were being brought into the covenant community. The principle, however, still stands: the covenant promises are for believers and their children.

3. The Bible views children as part of the covenant community. Very young children were present at covenant gatherings (Deut. 29:10-13; 2 Chron. 20:13; Joel 2:16). Jesus received children (even infants) as His people (Luke 18:15-16) while Paul stated that children of one believing parent are set apart to God (1 Cor. 7:14). In his letters to the Ephesians and Colossians, Paul addressed children as members of the church along with their parents. This doesn't mean that they are automatically saved; rather they are included as God's people and therefore subject to the sign and seal of inclusion.

4. In light of what we've seen, it shouldn't surprise us that *whole families* were baptized (Acts 10:47-48; 16:14-15, 30-33; 18:8; 1 Cor. 1:16). What was the basis for these baptisms? The answer is the faith of the head of the household. Just as Abraham's faith led to the circumcision of his household, so also the faith of these converts led to the baptism of their households. It's true that these texts do not mention children, but that's beside the point. While these households certainly included people who were capable of believing, it's irrelevant if the household formula continues from the Old Testament. The very fact that households are mentioned supports covenant continuity rather than discontinuity.

5. The new covenant is more inclusive than the old covenant. In the new covenant, unbelieving spouses are sanctified

by believing ones (1 Cor. 7:14) and women are baptized along with men (Gal. 3:27). If this is true, then it doesn't make sense to exclude those who were included under the old covenant sign of inclusion: believers and their children.

6. Refusing to apply circumcision to children meant breaking the covenant. In the Old Testament, this meant death (Gen. 17:13-14). Moses almost died because he did not circumcise his son (Exod. 4:24-26). While this is an extraordinary judgment, it still shows the seriousness of administering a sacrament to its proper recipients.

Questions for Review and Discussion

1. What are the Old Testament roots of baptism concerning purification?
2. What is baptism's connection with the remission of sins? Does it actually forgive sins?
3. What was the Old Testament counterpart of baptism as a rite of initiation? What were its sign and reality?
4. What happened to circumcision over the course of time? How was it fulfilled in Christ?
5. How does baptism point back to the Cross?
6. Briefly summarize the six reasons for baptizing believers and their children.

CHAPTER **13**

LORD'S SUPPER
Solemn Nurturing

The Lord's Supper is the sacrament of union and communion with our risen Savior. As such it includes an element of mystery. In the hands of sinful men, however, this mystery has led to misunderstanding, division, and superstition. In order to have a Biblical understanding of this sacrament, this chapter begins with Old Testament types, shows the transition into New Testament practice, interacts with differing views, and discusses the matter of proper participation ('fencing the table').

Type and Fulfillment

The gospels present the Last Supper as a Passover, one of the sacrificial meals of the Old Testament (Matt. 26:17-29; Mark 14:12-25; Luke 22:7-22). It involved sacrificing and eating a lamb, and spreading the blood on the doorframes of a home as a propitiation (Exod. 12). The Passover, however, wasn't the only sacrificial meal. The peace offerings of the

Mosaic Law involved sacrificing a part of an animal, giving a portion to the priest and eating the rest (Lev. 7:19-21, 28-34). In this way, God's people enjoyed communion with the Lord.

In the New Testament, these types and shadows find their fulfillment in Jesus Christ. He is the true Passover lamb who turns away the wrath of God (1 Cor. 5:7) and fulfills the entire sacrificial system (Heb. 10:1-7).

The Old Testament was also concerned with the concept of spiritual feeding. After delivering His people from slavery, God provided *manna*, bread from heaven, to sustain them during their time in the wilderness (Exod. 16). While His people didn't always appreciate this miraculous bread, they received it until they entered the land of Canaan.

After miraculously feeding a large group of people, Jesus referred to Himself as the true manna who gives life to the world (John 6:31-35). Then the imagery took an even more radical turn:

> Truly, truly, I say to you, unless you eat the flesh of the Son of Man and drink his blood, you have no life in you. Whoever feeds on my flesh and drinks my blood has eternal life, and I will raise him up on the last day. For my flesh is true food and my blood is true drink. Whoever feeds on my flesh and drinks my blood abides in me, and I in him (John 6:53-56).

How should we understand such language? His contemporaries thought they were listening to a cannibal! Moreover, what does this have to do with the Lord's Supper? It's interesting that Jesus used similar language at the last Passover with His disciples. He explained to them, 'This is my body which is given for you. ... This cup that is poured out for you is the new covenant in my blood' (Luke 22:19-20).

Does this mean that the Lord's Supper is really the body and blood of Christ? Some would say yes. On one hand, Roman Catholics believe that the bread and wine are transformed into the actual body and blood of Christ ('transubstantiation'). Such an understanding would make Jesus' words mean 'this is *becoming* my body'. On the other hand, Lutherans teach that Christ's body and blood are 'in, with, and under' the elements ('consubstantiation'). This theory would make Jesus say 'this *accompanies* my body'.

Others understand Jesus' words in a figurative sense. In Deuteronomy 16:3, unleavened bread is called 'the bread of affliction'. This bread didn't cause the Israelites' affliction; rather it *represented* their affliction. In a similar way, Jesus' words in John 6:53-56 and Luke 22:19-20 can be understood in a figurative way.

If his words are figurative, then does this mean they are only symbols of the body and blood of Christ? This is what many contemporary Christians believe. After all, Jesus also said, 'Do this in remembrance of me' (Luke 22:19-20). But did he mean *bare* remembrance? Was Jesus saying that He would be *absent* in the sacrament? The answer, of course, is no. Paul clearly taught the opposite in 1 Corinthians 10:16: 'The cup of blessing that we bless, is it not a participation in the blood of Christ? The bread that we break, is it not a participation in the body of Christ?' Here, the word translated as 'participation' is *koinonia* which elsewhere means 'fellowship' or 'communion'. While we often associate fellowship with a subjective feeling, the New Testament describes it as an objective state. As one of the goals of the gospel (1 John 1:3), it expresses unity in joy and suffering with Christ and His people (2 Cor. 1:7; 8:4; Phil. 3:10).

Yet this raises another question: How can God's people have fellowship with their risen Savior? The answer is by the power of the Holy Spirit who is Christ's presence in the world (John 14:26; 16:13-14). Therefore, remembrance speaks not of absence but of worship. It's a proclamation of the Lord's death until He comes (1 Corinthians 11:26). It points to the future glory of God's people when they feast with their risen Savior (Luke 22:18).

Fencing the Table

While the Lord's Supper is God's gracious gesture of communion, it involves some responsibility on the part of His people. There are a number of conditions that must be met in order to participate in this sacrament.

First the participant must be baptized. Here, the parallel with circumcision and Passover is instructive. According to Exodus 12:45, a foreigner could not eat the Passover until he was circumcised, the parallel Old Testament sacrament. Just as only those who had formally entered into Israel could partake of the Passover, so it follows that only those who formally enter the visible church can partake of the fulfillment of Passover.

Participation, however, requires more than baptism. It requires active membership in the Church of Jesus Christ. Paul wrote that 'because there is one bread, we who are many are one body, for we all partake of the one bread' (1 Cor. 10:17). Here, the body refers not to Christ's risen body but to the visible church (cf. 1 Cor. 12). Presbyterian churches do not consider themselves to be the only true churches, but recognize all churches that teach the gospel to be members of a larger body of Christ. Nevertheless, our churches receive many visitors who claim to be Christian but have not become members of their respective churches.

While a critique of this practice would take us beyond the scope of the chapter, it's fair to say that such people are not ready or willing to submit themselves to the formal oversight of a local church. Without such oversight, it would be difficult to determine their spiritual health. Since the sacrament is a *church* ordinance, it follows that only those who are in good and regular standing in a true church of Jesus Christ should be allowed to partake. Recognizing that this is a controversial point among Christians, it remains the practice of many Presbyterian churches.

Besides membership in the church of Christ, participation also requires something else. Only those who are capable of discernment and self-examination may participate in the sacrament. Concerning this matter, Paul instructed:

> Whoever, therefore, eats the bread or drinks the cup of the Lord in an unworthy manner will be guilty concerning the body and blood of the Lord. Let a person examine himself, then, and so eat of the bread and drink of the cup. For anyone who eats and drinks without discerning the body eats and drinks judgment on himself (1 Cor. 11:27-29).

This raises a number of questions. How does one differentiate between worthy and unworthy partaking? How much self-examination is necessary? What does it mean to discern the body? Some who are overly self-critical may read this and excuse themselves from the sacrament altogether! This is not Paul's goal. While everyone is unworthy by the mere fact that everyone is a sinner, the sacrament is still offered to sinners. Eating and drinking in an unworthy manner implies participating without 'repentance, love, and new obedience' (WSC 97). In the Corinthian church, this took the form of social and economic divisions that led to exclusion and drunkenness (1 Cor. 11:17-22). The oversight of the local church can provide counsel and assistance for those who struggle in these matters.

Self-examination involves the individual. One must take personal inventory before coming to the table. Self-examination, however, does not limit the advice or decisions of church officials. The church still has responsibility to judge its own, especially when its members are blind to their sins (1 Cor. 5:12).

Some Christians say that Paul was not excluding very young children from the Lord's Supper when he required self-examination. They argue that the warning was only for those mature enough to engage in self-reflection. This view, however, doesn't take into account the universal language 'whoever' (v. 27), 'let a person' (v. 28), 'anyone' (v. 29) that the apostle chose to describe the process of self-examination and discernment. These words testify to the fact that Paul was establishing a universal principle about participating in the sacrament.

So far we've discussed the moral conditions that must be met before coming to the table. What about doctrinal requirements? Here Paul spoke about 'discerning the body'. Is this a reference to the body as the church or the risen body of Christ? The former requires an understanding of being part of a larger community, while the latter requires an understanding of the sacrament and a fuller grasp of Biblical teaching. The answer isn't clear, but the possibilities are not mutually exclusive. Maturity involves both an understanding of doctrine and how it affects community living.

These are not trivial warnings. Members of the Church of Corinth were judged for their unworthy partaking of the sacrament (1 Cor. 11:30-31). While this judgment was extraordinary, it shows the gravity of taking the sacrament of solemn nurturing.

Questions for Review and Discussion

1. What are the Old Testament roots of the Lord's Supper concerning sacrificial meals? How were they fulfilled in Christ?

2. What are the Old Testament roots of the Lord's Supper concerning spiritual feeding? How were they fulfilled in Christ?

3. Should Christ's words concerning the bread and wine be taken literally or figuratively? Why or why not? Give examples of various approaches.

4. Briefly summarize the expectations for participants in the sacrament.

CHAPTER **14**

PRAYER
Daily Conversation

Prayer is not God's word or sacrament. Prayer is *our* word, our speaking to God. Yet prayer is still a means of grace. It is both a corporate and a private means of communion with God.

Prayer involves offering our desires to God. Jesus promised His disciples, 'Truly, truly, I say to you, whatever you ask of the Father in my name, he will give it to you' (John 16:23). Does this mean that God is going to give us whatever we request? That would turn Him into a genie! No, God gives us the desires that are agreeable to His good and perfect will. According to the Apostle John, 'This is the confidence that we have toward him, that if we ask anything according to his will he hears us' (1 John 5:14). How can we know His will? Read the Bible.

Some may ask how prayer is a means of grace. It's true that God is completely sovereign, but sometimes He condescends to accomplish His will through prayer. This is the expectation of the Psalmist who wrote, 'O Lord, in the morning you hear my voice; in the morning I prepare a sacrifice for you and watch' (Ps. 5:3). Paul concurred when he wrote this to the Colossian church: 'Continue steadfastly in prayer, being watchful in it with thanksgiving. At the same time, pray also for us, that God may open to us a door for the word, to declare the mystery of Christ' (Col. 4:2-3). Paul knew that his missionary efforts would be aided by prayer.

Nevertheless, some people are afraid to pray. They hear others speak beautiful prayers and become self-conscious. God, however, cares less about beautiful words than a humble heart. Jesus criticized the Jewish hypocrites for self-rewarding public prayers (Matt. 6:5) and the Gentiles for their 'heaped-up empty phrases and many words' (Matt. 6:7).

Knowing our weakness, Jesus taught His disciples a special prayer, the model for every individual prayer. We call it the *Lord's Prayer*. Its fullest form is found in the King James Version of Matthew 6:9-13:

> Our Father which art in heaven, Hallowed be thy name. Thy kingdom come. Thy will be done in earth, as it is in heaven. Give us this day our daily bread. And forgive us our debts, as we forgive our debtors. And lead us not into temptation, but deliver us from evil: For thine is the kingdom, and the power, and the glory, forever. Amen.

The Lord's prayer can be broken down as follows:

1. *Address* ('Our Father which art in heaven'). God wants us to address Him not out of fear but out of security, as a child speaks to His father. Christians are His adopted children who can cry out to Him, 'Abba! Father!' (Rom. 8:15). This speaks not only of relationship but intimacy. Even though God is in the eternal realm of heaven, He's a personal father who's always close at hand.

Notice, however, that the prayer does not begin, 'My Father' but 'Our Father'. In the earliest meetings of the church, 'the prayers' were a vital element alongside the apostolic teaching, the fellowship, and 'the breaking of bread' or Lord's Supper (Acts 2:42). Later the church prayed for boldness and received a positive answer (Acts 4:23-31). God's people must never lose sight of the *church* when praying to the Father.

2. *Adoration* ('Hallowed be thy name'). This is the chief end of man (WSC 1). God's people are to exalt the Lord before they offer up their concerns. God's name describes His entire being. 'O LORD, our Lord, how majestic is your name in all the earth. You have set your glory above the heavens' (Ps. 8:1). This first petition not only reminds us of our need to adore God, but moves us to make His name known to others. In the words of one psalmist, 'May God be gracious to us and bless us and make his face to shine upon us, that your way may be known on earth, your saving power among all nations. Let the peoples praise you, O God, let the peoples praise you!' (Ps. 67:1-3).

3. *Advancement* ('Thy kingdom come, Thy will be done in earth as it is in heaven'). Jesus said, 'My kingdom is not of this world' (John 18:36). It's a future reality, even though the Church is a present manifestation of that reality (Matt. 16:18-19). It's an appeal for the second coming of Christ, when all sin will be removed, all tears will be wiped away, and God's people will be ushered into glory (Rev. 21:4). At the same time, it's a plea for the spread of the gospel and the growth of the Church until that glorious day arrives. At the most basic level, however, it's a petition for contentment, knowing that God's will is better than our own.

4. *Provision* ('Give us this day our daily bread'). This petition focuses on our daily dependence upon God. Matthew 6:31-33

shows how this follows the previous petition: 'Therefore do not be anxious, saying, "What shall we eat?" or "What shall we drink?" or "What shall we wear?" For the Gentiles seek after all these things, and your heavenly Father knows that you need them all. But seek first the kingdom of God and his righteousness, and all these things will be added to you.' In the Lord's prayer, 'these things' are symbolized by the image of bread, daily nourishment for the majority of mankind. Agur the son of Jakeh echoed this sentiment in the Old Testament: 'Give me neither poverty or riches; feed me with the food that is needful for me' (Prov. 30:8). This is a prayer for what is basic instead of glorious. The latter will come later.

5. *Confession* ('Forgive us our debts, as we forgive our debtors'). This petition focuses on the need for forgiveness. What greater debt could man have than his sin? How could he possibly pay it? He can't, but forgiveness is free. The Apostle John reminds us that, 'If we confess our sins, he is faithful and just to forgive us our sins and cleanse us from all unrighteousness' (1 John 1:9). Here, justice and mercy find their intersection in the work of Christ. His obedience made it possible for God to *justly* forgive our sins. This should spur God's people to forgive each other, because they have been forgiven first.

6. *Protection* ('And lead us not into temptation, but deliver us from evil'). While confession leads to repentance, change can be difficult. This petition concerns our ongoing struggle, the temptations of the world, the flesh, and the devil. Jesus understood our plight when He prayed, 'I do not ask that you take them out of the world, but that you keep them from the evil one' (John 17:15). Notice that He did not pray for our *removal* from the world. The reason for this is that God uses circumstances in the world, the flesh, and the devil to test our faith and to refine us more and more as His

people. The ultimate deliverance will take place when the Kingdom of God comes in its fullness. Then the new heavens and earth will come (Rev. 21:1), God's people will be glorified (1 Cor. 15:52) and the devil will receive his due (Rev. 20:10).

7. *Doxology* ('For thine is the kingdom, and the power, and the glory, forever. Amen.'). This is a recognition of God's supremacy over all things. The fact that nothing in the universe can thwart His plans should give His people the greatest assurance of all.

Questions for Review and Discussion

1. What does prayer involve?
2. How is prayer a means of grace?
3. Why are some people reluctant to pray?
4. Briefly summarize the Lord's Prayer, explaining how to best understand each part.

APPENDIX I

Glossary

Adam	The first human being and federal head of the human race who was created innocent but chose evil. His sin rendered all of mankind guilty and corrupt.
Apostle	Literally a 'sent one' appointed by Christ and given unique authority as His official representative.
Baptism	The sacrament of purification and initiation into the covenant community involving the sign of water.
Biblical Authority	The belief that the Bible is the ultimate standard to measure all other standards (e.g., reason, experience, tradition).
Biblical Canon	The closed collection of sixty-six books.
Biblical Inerrancy	The belief that the Bible is without error.
Biblical Infallibility	The belief that the Bible cannot be proven wrong.

Biblical Inspiration	The belief that the writers were overseen by God to the extent that God is the author of the Bible.
Circumcision	The Old Testament forerunner of baptism whereby through the cutting of the foreskin God's people were marked as being in a covenant relationship with Him.
Church	The assembly of God's people throughout the Bible, expanding from one family, to one nation, to people from every nation.
Circumstance of Worship	A situation or factor that facilitates public worship.
Congregationalist Polity	The localized form of government whereby the church is ruled by the congregation.
Covenant	A legal relationship between two or more parties that involves blessings and curses.
Covenant Mediator	One who reconciles two hostile parties in a covenant. In the covenant of grace, Christ does so at the cost of His own life.
Covenant of Grace	The covenant between God and His people whereby salvation is granted to those who place their faith in the covenant mediator, Jesus Christ.
Covenant of Works	The covenant between God and Adam whereby eternal life would have been granted to the latter and his descendants had he obeyed perfectly.
Creation	God's work of bringing the heavens and the earth into existence.
Crucifixion	Christ's death on the cross as the ultimate sacrifice for the sins of His people.
Deacon	The church officer who assists the presbyters by providing for the temporal needs of God's people so the work of the ministry of the word and prayer is not hindered.

Dialogical Principle of Worship	The conversation between God speaking and His people responding in public worship.
Element of Worship	Something that must be done in public worship.
Episcopal Polity	The hierarchical form of government whereby the church is ruled by bishops.
Eternality	God's infinity expressed in time.
Faith, Saving	God's gift to sinners whereby they receive and rest upon Christ alone for their salvation.
Form of Worship	The way an element can be expressed in public worship.
Free Will	The ability to make choices according to one's nature.
General Revelation	God's self-disclosure in the natural world, evidenced by the powers of observation.
Gospel	Literally the 'good news' of God's salvation of sinners by the obedience and sacrifice of His Son, Jesus Christ.
Grace	God's favorable disposition to undeserving sinners.
Heaven	The realm of endless blessing and destination of God's people.
Hell	The realm of endless suffering and destination of Satan, his minions, and people who have not been saved by Christ.
Holiness	God's attribute describing His purity and perfection. Partially communicated to mankind.
Holy Spirit	The third person of the Trinity who applies the blessings of Christ to His people.
Holy Tradition	A worship approach where tradition is more important than Scripture.

Image of God	The description of mankind as God's children who were created to reflect His attributes to the lesser creation.
Imputation	The crediting of Adam's sin to his descendants or Christ's righteousness and sacrifice to His people.
Incomprehensibility	God's attribute describing His inability to be known apart from revelation.
Incarnation	The event of the Second Person of the Trinity becoming human and resulting in the God-man.
Infinity	God's attribute describing His limitlessness.
Irresistible Grace	The Holy Spirit calling and awakening the people God chose and Christ saved.
Israel	God's people who were constituted as a nation at Sinai and ruled the land of Canaan. In the New Testament, the church is called the Israel of God.
Jesus Christ	The second person of the Trinity who became human, lived a sinless life, suffered, died, and was resurrected for His people.
Justification	God's act of forgiving sin and declaring a person as righteous in His sight, based on the imputation of Christ's righteousness to that person. Received by faith alone.
Law	God's means of expressing His righteous will for His image-bearers. Aspects include ceremonies that pointed to Christ, regulations for the nation of Israel, and rules for all times and places.
Limited Atonement	Christ's sacrifice for the people God gave Him.

Lord's Supper	The sacrament of communion between God and His people involving the signs of bread and wine.
Love	God's greatest attribute communicated to mankind.
Means of Grace	The channels God uses to communicate the work of salvation to His people: preaching, sacraments, and prayer.
New Covenant	The covenant instituted through Christ where God's people of every tribe and nation are saved from their sins. Supercedes the Old Covenant.
New Testament	Twenty-seven books of the Bible beginning with the Gospel of Matthew and ending with the Revelation.
Normative Principle of Worship	A common approach to public worship that permits anything not forbidden in the Bible.
Old Covenant	The covenant instituted at Sinai where God made Israel into His nation. Superceded by the New Covenant.
Old Testament	Thirty-nine books of the Bible beginning with Genesis and ending with the Prophecy of Malachi.
Omnipresence	God's infinity expressed in space.
Perseverance of the Saints	The understanding that the people who were chosen by the Father, saved by the Son, and called by the Spirit cannot lose their salvation and will endure to the end.
Prayer	A means of grace involving man's communication with God.
Preaching	A means of grace involving the proclamation of Christ and all His benefits to God's people.

Presbyter	Church officers that include word ministers and ruling elders.
Presbyterian Polity	The interconnected form of government whereby the church is ruled by presbyters.
Prophet	A person who spoke or wrote special revelation.
Proto-evangel	The first occurrence of the gospel declaring that the offspring of the woman will defeat the power of Satan.
Providence	God's work of preserving and governing everything He created.
Regulative Principle of Worship	An approach to public worship that only allows for what God commands in the Bible.
Resurrection	Christ's rising from the dead on the third day. Confirms the Father's acceptance of His sacrifice, demonstrates that death has been defeated, and assures God's people of their future resurrection unto eternal life.
Righteousness	God's attribute describing His justice. Partially communicated to mankind.
Sacraments	Means of grace involving sensory signs and seals that represent and confirm the benefits of salvation to God's people.
Sanctification	God's progressive action of renewing the image of God and causing His people to grow in holiness.
Satan	A spiritual creature also known as the Devil who successfully tempted Adam into breaking the covenant of works and continues to tempt mankind.
Second Adam	Christ's role as federal head of a new human race. His obedience renders His people righteous in the eyes of God.

Sin	A violation of God's law. Originated in the Garden of Eden when Adam broke the covenant of works. Results in guilt, corruption, death, and eternal condemnation.
Sovereignty	God's attribute describing His full control over all things. Partially communicated to mankind.
Special Revelation	God's self-disclosure in His supernatural word, the Bible.
Substitutionary Sacrifice	The system of offering animals to die in place of God's sinful people. Fulfilled by Christ on the cross.
Total Depravity	The condition whereby sin infects every part of humanity, rendering a person incapable of choosing God.
Trinity	God's attribute where He is one God in three persons: Father, Son, and Holy Spirit. The expression of God's love in eternity and collaboration of God's saving plan in history.
Unconditional Election	God's choosing His people apart from any foreseen qualities such as faith or obedience.

APPENDIX II

Sample Liturgy

A. We *prepare* our hearts

Element	Element Category	Justification	Participant	Action
Silent Prayer	Prayer	Psalm 62:1	People speak (silently)	We silently prepare for worship.

B. God *calls* us

Element	Element Category	Justification	Participant	Action
God's Greeting	Reading of the Word	Revelation 1:4	God speaks (through minister)	God greets us as His people.
Call to Worship	Reading of the Word	Psalm 95:1-2	God speaks (through minister)	God calls us into His presence.
Song of Approach	Congrega-tional Song	Psalm 134	People speak (unison)	We approach Him in song.
Prayer of Invocation	Prayer	Psalm 145:18	People speak (through minister)	We call upon His name in prayer.

C. God *cleanses* us

Element	Element Category	Justification	Participant	Action
Reading of the Law	Reading of the Word	Nehemiah 8:1-3	God speaks (through minister)	God's righteousness is displayed in the reading of His law. This exposes our sinfulness and need for confession.
Prayer of Confession	Prayer	Nehemiah 9:1-3; Psalm 51	People speak (through minister or corporately)	We confess our sins and ask for God's forgiveness.
Assurance of Pardon	Reading of the Word	1 John 1:9	God speaks (through minister)	God forgives our sins and assures of His mercy through the gospel.
Baptism	Sacrament	1 Corinthians 1:16-17;* Acts 2:38-41	God speaks (through minister)	In occasional services, our forgiveness is also signified and sealed in baptism.

*Acts 2:41 (baptism) is directly followed by a description of church worship. Likewise, 1 Corinthians concerns problems associated with worship (baptism in Chapter 1, Lord's Supper in Chapters 10 and 11).

C. God *cleanses* us (cont.)

Element	Element Category	Justification	Participant	Action
Public Profession of Faith	Vow	Romans 10:9-10; 1 Timothy 6:12	People speak (individual)	In occasional services, individual adult(s) or children confirm their cleansing through membership vows.
Song of Reconciliation	Congregational Song	Psalm 103:8	People speak (unison)	We respond in song.

D. God *connects* us

Element	Element Category	Justification	Participant	Action
Prayer of Intercession (with Lord's Prayer)	Prayer	Psalm 119:17-18; 1 Timothy 2:1-4; Matthew 6:9-13	People speak (through minister)	Having been cleansed and connected to the Body of Christ, we approach the throne of grace, asking for intercession.

E. God *consecrates* us

Element	Element Category	Justification	Participant	Action
Sermon Text	Reading of the Word	1 Timothy 4:13	God speaks (through minister)	God responds by consecrating His people through the reading and preaching of His Word.
Sermon	Preaching of the Word	Romans 10:14-17; 1 Timothy 4:13	God speaks (through minister)	
Prayer of Application	Prayer	Acts 20:36; Ephesians 3:14-21	People speak (through minister)	We pray for God to apply these truths to us.
Song of Consecration	Congregational Song	Ephesians 5:19; Colossians 3:16	People speak (unison)	We respond to God's grace.
Confession of Faith	Vow	Romans 10:9-10; Hebrews 12:22-23	People speak (unison)	We confess our faith through an ecumenical creed.

F. God *communes* with us

Element	Element Category	Justification	Participant	Action
Lord's Supper Words of Institution	Sacrament	1 Corinthians 11:23-26	God speaks (through minister)	Having consecrated us, God now shares a covenant meal with us. We respond in prayer and song.
Meaning and Nature	Sacrament	Luke 22:15-20; 1 Corinthians 10:16-17	God speaks (through minister)	
Fencing the Table	Sacrament	1 Corinthians 11:27-29	God speaks (through minister)	
Prayer	Prayer	Luke 22:19	People speak (through minister)	
Communion	Sacrament	Acts 20:7,11	God speaks (through minister)	
Song of Communion	Congregational Song	Matthew 26:30	People speak (unison)	

G. God *dismisses*

Element	Element Category	Justification	Participant	Action
Offering Exhortation	Reading of the Word	Psalm 96:8	God speaks (through minister)	Having received God's grace, we respond in gratitude through the giving of our tithes and offerings.
Collection	Offering	1 Corinthians 16:1-2	People speak (silently)	
Offertory Prayer	Prayer	Acts 2:42	People speak (through minister)	
Doxology	Congregational Song	Revelation 7:10-12	People speak (unison)	We glorify God for His blessings.
God's Blessing	Reading of the Word	Numbers 6:24-27; Hebrews 13:20-21	God speaks (through minister)	God places His name of ownership upon us.

Christian Focus Publications

Our mission statement –

STAYING FAITHFUL

In dependence upon God we seek to impact the world through literature faithful to His infallible Word, the Bible. Our aim is to ensure that the Lord Jesus Christ is presented as the only hope to obtain forgiveness of sin, live a useful life and look forward to heaven with Him.

Our books are published in four imprints:

CHRISTIAN FOCUS

Popular works including biographies, commentaries, basic doctrine and Christian living.

CHRISTIAN HERITAGE

Books representing some of the best material from the rich heritage of the church.

MENTOR

Books written at a level suitable for Bible College and seminary students, pastors, and other serious readers. The imprint includes commentaries, doctrinal studies, examination of current issues and church history.

CF4•K

Children's books for quality Bible teaching and for all age groups: Sunday school curriculum, puzzle and activity books; personal and family devotional titles, biographies and inspirational stories – because you are never too young to know Jesus!

Christian Focus Publications Ltd,
Geanies House, Fearn, Ross-shire,
IV20 1TW, Scotland, United Kingdom.
www.christianfocus.com
blog.christianfocus.com